— ♦ —

Accepting

Bereavement

— ♦ —

Accepting Bereavement

The Healing Process of Grief

Presented to

_____

by

A Message from
the Heart

Accepting Bereavement

The Healing Process of Grief

Nashville, Tennessee

Contents

Foreword

by Jim Bill McInteer

*I*ts purpose is twofold. Someone wanted you to know they cared and gave you this book as an expression of their deep concern. *Accepting Bereavement* also comes to you personally to help you deal with a devastating experience. It serves as a guideline to instruct you with the words of those who have traveled the path of loss which lies ahead for you.

You hurt. Someone so precious to you has expired. Will there be a brighter day? Yes, yes, yes—it will come and these words can greatly aid. Knowing these capable writers and their rich experiences, I believe their words will bring peace to your heart. I base this on the fact that I've preached the gospel of Christ for 60 years and have been a part of at least 1,000 funerals. These writers know whereof they speak.

When we deal with death, we deal with the inevitable. I may never need a book on travel, on cooking, or on mechanical drawing – but there is no escaping my rendezvous with death. It is our one undeniable encounter. In an effort to help you meet this universal experience, we put at your disposal these uplifting words. May they be a blessing to all as either early or late in life we must learn to "accept bereavement." May God use this tender message to His glory and your peace of mind.

Believers have found more comfort in this
psalm than in any words ever written.
May you find comfort here:

A Psalm of Comfort

*T*he LORD is my shepherd; I shall not want. He
maketh me to lie down in green pastures: He
leadeth me beside the still waters. He restoreth my
soul: He leadeth me in the paths of righteousness for
His name's sake.

Yea, though I walk through the valley of the shadow of
death, I will fear no evil: for Thou art with me; Thy rod
and Thy staff they comfort me.

Thou preparest a table before me in the presence of
mine enemies: Thou anointest my head with oil; my
cup runneth over.

Surely goodness and mercy shall follow me all the days
of my life: and I will dwell in the house of the LORD for
ever.

PSALM 23

(KJV)

When You Lose One You Love

by Helen M. Young

*W*hen you lose your loved one in death, Jesus is there to comfort and strengthen you with His love. Just as His heart was touched by Mary's and Martha's grief at the death of Lazarus, so He will be with you.

Jesus revealed His compassionate heart with His own tears as he stood by the tomb. I am glad that John records the shortest verse in the Bible, "Jesus wept." The perfect son of God cried. You can be sure that your pain and tears do not go unnoticed by Him. In the Beatitudes He said, "Blessed are those who mourn, for they will be comforted." Jesus comforts us when we mourn.

> *"Blessed are those who mourn, for they will be comforted."*
>
> Matthew 5:4

Tears are the language of our soul to express our own grief, just as they were for Jesus. God made our tear ducts and the glands which regulate our moods. He knows how deeply we are grieved, and He has provided tears as a means for us to vent our emotions. Tears are a necessary relief.

But we can be sure we never cry alone. His heart is touched with our grief. He will never leave us and His loving arms are around us to comfort and strengthen.

When Paul pens those beautiful words in Romans 8:35-39 he lists seventeen things that cannot separate you and me from God's love in Christ: trouble, hardship, persecution, famine, nakedness, danger or sword. "No, in all these things we are more than conquerors through Him who loved us. For I am convinced that neither death nor life, neither angels nor demons, neither the present nor the future, nor any powers, neither height nor depth, nor anything else in all creation, will be able to separate us from the love of God that is in Christ Jesus our Lord."

Midst the unspeakable pain and the inevitable questions surrounding our loss, we are strengthened to know that God shares our sorrow and that He is near to comfort.

> *Could it be that loneliness is given to us as a reminder that this world was never intended to be our home and the things of this world were never intended to satisfy us?*
>
> –Verdell Davis
> *Let Me Grieve*
> *But Not Forever*

At first we are in almost a state of shock which may make us feel numb as if we had been under anesthesia. Usually there is some weeping, but we carry on with the tasks that accompany death. We greet friends and relatives, we make decisions, we seek to comfort our children. To others we may be considered very strong, but in reality our heart is breaking. To be comforted in the face of grief we must not refuse to face the loss. We must mourn. Faith and tears do mix. In fact weeping is a most effective medicine.

The healing process of grief requires a series of tasks:

- We must accept reality.

- We must experience the pain. This may include dealing with resentment, depression, fatigue, etc.

- We must let go of the past.

- We must eventually reinvest our energy into the meaningful future. The God of scripture is always calling us into our tomorrow.

Grief is like the ocean tides. It comes in waves. Just when you feel you are doing better, a wave of grief will sweep over you that is overwhelming. You weep as you did in the initial days of grief. It may be triggered by a song you hear or a letter you receive. It may be a worship service that you always shared or an anniversary date, or any one of thousands of precious memories. The tides of grief go in and out.

> *Grief is like the ocean tides. It comes in waves.*

At times your thoughts are filled with the details of the death, the funeral, your loss. Later there will be times when these are replaced by memories of the joys you shared throughout the years. Eventually the tides of grief will be less turbulent and the periods in between will be longer. There will be ebb and flow.

The assurance we long for in our grief is that God is present, that he has not forsaken us; that He knows what we are experiencing and that He cares and will comfort. The Bible is so positive on each of these longings.

> "May the Lord Jesus Christ Himself and God our Father, who loved us and by His grace gave us eternal encouragement and good hope, encourage your hearts and strengthen you in every good deed and word."
>
> 2 Thessalonians 2:16

"So do not fear, for I am with you; do not be dismayed, for I am your God. I will strengthen you and help you; I will uphold you with my righteous right hand . . . For I am the Lord your God, who takes hold of your right hand and says to you, Do not fear; I will help you" (Isaiah 41:10,13).

Christ said, "And surely I am with you always, to the very end of the age" (Matthew 28:20).

"For the Lord comforts His people and will have compassion on His afflicted ones... 'Can a mother forget the baby at her breast and have no compassion on the child she has borne? Though she may forget, I will not forget you!' " (Isaiah 49:13,15).

4

God comforts us through His Word. We need to hunger and thirst for it and find the solace God provides there. Randy Becton said that in his sorrow he "lived in the Psalms" and learned that he could trust God with the full range of his emotions.

God also comforts us through people. Comfort comes when the bereaved know they are not alone. Friends who will listen, who will say, "Would you like to talk about it?" or "Tell me how things are" are thoughtful, loving friends who help us begin the process of facing reality and of acceptance. Friends who say, "I will pray for you every day," are a blessing. Friends who talk too much or try to change the subject are not comforting.

The dear friend or relative who hugs you and helps you, prays with you and cries with you is Christ's love in human form. The phone call, the cards and letters they send, the food that comes to your home and the flowers are all His gifts. Remember that the hands that bring you comfort and encouragement are His hands and He is present and His love is constant. As one grieving parent said, "The hurt goes deep, but His love goes deeper."

> *The dear friend or relative who hugs you and helps you, prays with you and cries with you is Christ's love in human form.*

Truly the best news the world has ever heard is the news of the resurrection of Jesus Christ—because it is true. Because it proves the deity of our Lord. It proves that we can be justified before God. Paul said that Jesus "was delivered over to death for our sins and was raised to life for our justification" (Romans 4:25).

And the resurrection of Jesus Christ is also evidence for our own resurrection and of a life with Jesus in glory beyond the grave. As He said, "And if I go and prepare a place for you, I will come back and take you to be with Me that you also may be where I am" (John 14:3). The end of this life is not a question mark—it is Jesus. We shall be with Him. This hope of eternal life is our comfort as grief begins its healing work.

> "I believe in our periods of deepest grief, we can trust God to prepare someone to come our way to speak a word of love or encouragement to us, or perhaps to be present with us, to weep with us, or to walk with us in silence and faith."
>
> – Zig Ziglar
> *Confessions of a Grieving Christian*

Death is not a wall. It is a door into a larger, fuller life. God and Christ will be there for eternity and there will be no more tears, death will be no more, neither will there be crying or pain, but "pleasures forevermore."

From all that the Bible discloses, we will not lose our identities in heaven. When Moses and Elijah came back from the dead at the transfiguration, they had not lost their identities. Paul says, "Then shall I know, even as also I am known." And from Paul's words there is no delay between death and the life to come. He uses the phrase, "Absent from the body, at home with the Lord." Later he wrote of his "desire to depart and be with Christ, for that is far better."

What a blessed hope, to anticipate being with our loved one for an eternity of joy in a land that is fairer than day! Jesus said that God had sent Him to heal the brokenhearted. Someday you will be able to smile and say, "My broken heart is healed." Someday.

It Is Well With My Soul

Horatio Spafford was a successful Chicago attorney with a wife and four daughters. He had planned a family vacation to Europe in 1873 but was held up by urgent business. Spafford decided to send his wife and daughters on as scheduled and catch up with them as soon as business was settled. Halfway across the Atlantic the cruise ship was struck by another ship and sank in only twelve minutes. All four of Spafford's daughters lost their lives. As Spafford made his way to Wales to meet his grieving wife, he penned the words to this hymn of unshakable trust in God.

> When peace like a river, attendeth my way,
> When sorrows like sea billows roll,
> Whatever my lot, Thou hast taught me to say,
> "It is well, it is well with my soul."
>
> Tho' Satan should buffet, tho' trials should come,
> Let this blest assurance control,
> That Christ hath regarded my helpless estate
> And hath shed His own blood for my soul.
>
> And, Lord, haste the day when the faith shall be sight,
> The clouds be rolled back as a scroll,
> The trump shall resound and the Lord shall descend,
> "Even so" it is well with my soul.

When Death Takes Someone You Love

by M. Norvel Young

*T*he crushing blows of life's storms strike heavy upon us in the passing of a loved one. Some fall beneath their sorrows and are defeated. Others weather the fury of the storm and come through stronger. For them there seems to be a new strength and depth to their character after the storm is past.

They do not deny the pain of separation of one so dear. Love remembers the years of joy in nearness. But the deep roots of their Christian faith give them strength. They see the outstretched arms of their Savior as he says, "Come, all you who are weary and burdened, and I will give you rest" (Matthew 11:28). They know that Christ came to heal the brokenhearted. By faith they find in Christ courage, trust and hope for the future.

> *Afflictions, though they seem severe, in mercy oft are sent.*
>
> – Charles H. Spurgeon

Death is a part of life, and accepting sorrow is a part of life that all must learn. But all around us are others who also suffer and we are needed as comforters. Costen Harrell has said, "In the valley of deep shadows and in the teeth of the storm we hear a divine voice speaking to us ever so tenderly, and yet in strong clear accents, saying, 'Stand upright on your feet'. The spirit of

8

Christ imparts the courage to stand erect when the tempest is most severe."

As the bird can sing in the midst of the storm because she knows she has wings to carry her upward when the branch breaks, so the brokenhearted can find peace in sorrow because of the confidence that underneath are the everlasting arms that can sustain and comfort. When other helpers fail and comforts flee, He who changes not abides with us. We can trust Him, "who is able to do immeasurably more than all we ask or imagine ..." (Ephesians 3:20).

> *We are and always will be operating in an imperfect world. But we do have a perfect example.*
>
> – James F. Hind

A trusting heart will know sorrow but not despair, and will in that sorrow believe that "in all things God works for the good of those who love Him ..." (Romans 8:28). To trustingly commit ourselves and our ways to His care brings peace. We can let go and let God. We can know that in our weakness, He is our strength; in our sorrow, He is our comfort. We need to consciously and daily commit ourselves to His care in trusting faith.

We believe our dear one lives on, that beyond death there is a beautiful eternity with God. As the Strait of Gibraltar seems to close as a gate before the ship as it travels west in the Mediterranean, so death seems to close us in from life. But as the broad expanses of the Atlantic open wide beyond the strait, so do the beautiful vistas of eternity open wide to the Christian beyond death.

This is the blessed hope of the Christian: "In My Father's house are many rooms; if it were not so, I would have told you. I am going there to prepare a place for you." (John 14:2). How blessed is the assurance that "when He appears, we shall be like Him ..." (I John 3:2).

> "... *in all these things we are more than conquerors...*"
>
> Romans 8:37

Death is not disaster but a blessing. It is the gracious provision of God that our spirits might dwell with Him forever. This is our hope.

To Comfort You

May these suggestions help you as you meet your soul's deep need in time of sorrow:

1. Graciously accept the sympathy of others. Sometimes they will not know how to express themselves well, but their love is sincere and you help them and yourself in leaning on them for a time. Christians are taught to weep with those who weep. "We share our mutual woes, our mutual burdens bear, and often for each other flows the sympathizing tear."

2. Recognize that the pain will grow more bearable. The pain of sorrow is acute, but time will help, or rather we should say God will help and He uses time to heal our hurts.

3. Turn to the Bible with renewed thirst. "I opened the old, old Bible, and looked at a page of Psalms, till the wintry sea of my troubles were soothed as by summer calms; for the words that

have helped so many, and the ages have made more dear, seemed new in their power to comfort, as they brought me their words of cheer."

4. Tap the power of prayer. As Tennyson said, "There is more wrought by prayer than this world dreams of." It is not an accident that the old hymn contains this phrase: "What a friend we have in Jesus, all our sins and griefs to bear." Pour out your heart to God. Jesus understands. "For I am convinced that neither death nor life, neither angels nor demons, neither the present nor the future, nor any powers, neither height nor depth, nor anything else in all creation, will be able to separate us from the love of God that is in Christ Jesus our Lord" (Romans 8:38,39).

5. Be even more faithful in worship. Some make the mistake of withdrawing from others, closing the blinds and locking the door. The wise Christian, however, knows that worshipping with others who have also suffered will help. The solace of worship will be a strength and comfort.

6. Look for others who need your help. Work is a blessing in overcoming sorrow. There is no substitute for getting busy helping others. The best way to honor the dead is to serve the living. Cultivate a willingness to stop and help others rather than pass by on the other side. Jesus will be with you and you will be able to say with Paul: "I can do everything through Him who gives me strength (Philippians 4:13).

A Prayer of Grief

Lord God, hear my prayer,

My struggle, as You know,
 is with loss.

Through death, I've lost
 a significant part of me.

I'm left here wondering,
 striving to pick up the pieces
 weary of the task.

Like a bird whose nest has been robbed,
 I feel lost, alone
 and purposeless.

Some days, I'm better —
 energized, feeling alive
 ready to engage life.

Other days, I regress—
 despondent, feeling lonely,
 ladened with sorrow.

I'm told to get out more, to snap out of it,
 to move on,
 to quit hurting.

And I wish I could. But this work
        of grieving takes time,
        for my life is slowly taking
        new shape, new directions.

And such a process, like birth,
        takes time, and the kind
        assistance of others, and You.

Lord, I appreciate the memories,
        those private, sacred treasures
        that bring me tears and laughter.

I thank You for Your Word,
        replete with stories of other grievers,
        and comforting phrases
        of Your love.

I praise You for those special friends
        who give me space to hurt,
        who ask me to recall precious stories,
        who refuse to let me despair alone.

Such gifts, Lord, keep me going,
        and remind me
        that tomorrow, like yesterday and today,
        is in Your capable, caring hands.

Lord God, hear my prayer.

                                        –Virgil Fry

Grief Work

by Randy Becton

*B*ereavement, the universal crisis, strikes an average of two American families per minute. Active bereavement involves at least a million Americans at any one time. We will experience this problem in our personal lives, as well as deal with it countless times in the lives of others. No other human knows the deep ache a person is experiencing when he or she loses a loved one. Grieving is universal, but also so personal and individual.

> *Grief is like a long valley, a winding valley where any bend may reveal a totally new landscape.*
>
> – C. S. Lewis
> *A Grief Observed*

The primary idea expressed by the word bereavement is the loss, taking away, of death, of someone or something very precious to an individual. Nearly every feeling known to man can be involved in the crisis of bereavement. The loss of a loved one is a psychological amputation. A part of one's world of meaning and identity has been cut off. The response of a person to this loss is one form or another of grief, depending on the nature of the relationship and the mental health of the individual. Bereavement is often closely connected with feelings of loneliness and depression. Grief is a very painful experience because it involves the breaking of many deep emotional ties and the disruption of habitual patterns of living.

14

The process of bereavement may take many legitimate forms with different people. But in all of them there are these basic characteristics:

1. Painful recollection of the deceased person, with,

2. An increasing capacity to "tolerate" the image rather than a compulsion to avoid or repress everything into the subconscious.

3. Involved in the nature of bereavement is the biblical phrase: "Blessed are they that mourn for they shall be comforted." This verse gives us reason to believe that there is a meaningful way in which bereavement may be dealt with, resulting in good.

Symptoms of Grief

Grief has a normal set of symptoms which must be understood and accepted as a part of dealing with the process. Grief typically shows itself by marked physical distress. This could include such feelings as tightness in the throat, shortness of breath, a feeling of emptiness in the abdomen, a lack of energy, and severe feelings of inner tension or pain.

A symptom of *acute* grief is the complaint that things seem to be unreal. There is a feeling of increased emotional distance from people. There is also a sense of preoccupation with the image or memory of the deceased. Many people will idealize the deceased person, sometimes beyond recognition.

Another common symptom of grief is a feeling of guilt. Bereaved persons are likely to indicate that they have failed to do the right thing by the deceased person. They accuse themselves of negligence or exaggerate minor omissions.

Another type of symptom is a feeling of being cold, irritable, or even hostile toward others.

Handling Grief

Dr. Eric Lindemann, an expert on grief, speaks of what he calls "grief work". By this he means the necessity of working through feelings of pain and loss and coming to the place where you discover ways in which you can go on without the deceased person. A large part of this "grief work" is the process of dealing with the memory of the deceased.

You may begin by talking about the deceased in a very idealized manner and gradually proceed to a more realistic view of the relationship as you work further back from the time of death into more remote experiences. This is accompanied by a marked release of tension. One of the most important aspects of this process is that you share your feelings with another person in whom you have deep trust and confidence. This person needs to be one who offers acceptance and understanding, gives freedom but allows for some dependence, and one who feels a sense of responsibility to help you through the process.

Conclusion

Grief is a normal human experience which must be confronted, but can be conquered with time, friendships, and prayer.

Excerpted and adapted from
A Friend's Grief: How You Can Help
by Randy Becton

The Letter

by Dorris Haase

The letter lay, fragile and stained on top of the pile. It was hard going through my mother's things. Missing her was still so new. I looked at the date. It had been written by a friend to my mother shortly after my father died.

"Dear One," it began, "it hurts so terribly, doesn't it? Accept the pain if you can. Say, 'Yes, because I have loved and now lost, I must cry for a while. I must hold this ache of loneliness within myself and say, this is the price I pay for having loved. I will accept this price and pay it in gratitude for the love I was blessed to know, for I would not have wanted to be without that love. I will pay this price, God, and I thank You for the wonderful years we shared.'

"I think He must have cried on the day that His son hung dead on the cross, don't you think so? Don't you think that because He, too, is familiar with tears, dear friend, He is especially close to you right now?

"I weep with you, and my love surrounds you. Please write and let me know your plans, and if there is anything at all I can do to help."

I folded the letter and slipped it back into the envelope, grateful for this healing message from the past.

"Thank you for the wonderful years, Mom," I whispered. "Of all the women in the world, I'm so lucky *you* were the one God gave me. Yes, it was worth the price."

God Has His Greatest Successes Among the Brokenhearted

by Bailey McBride

*L*oss is a common denominator in human experiences. Jesus tells three parables in Luke 15 to illustrate the seriousness of losing someone special. The parables talk about a lost sheep, a lost coin and a lost son. In the stories Jesus tells, what is lost is eventually recovered. Many human losses, however, cannot be recovered. I have read that the death of a child has the greatest repercussions on a family even when the child is an older adult. Divorce ranks among the most painful losses for all those involved—parents, children and mates. The loss of a home or personal possessions, no matter what the cause, grieves most people. Losing wealth, reputation or standing, or a job takes a tremendous toll on those who are affected.

Since loss is such a common experience, we all need to work on the attitudes and strategies for going through a loss with the least possible damage to our hearts, our minds, and our souls.

Realize the Significance of the Loss

It is healthy to take time to understand fully the extent and significance of the loss. Although we may feel violated and angry that someone has broken into our home and taken our prized possessions, we eventually realize that we can cope with the loss of "things". Even when we experience a rupture in a significant relationship, we can work through the feelings and understand that we can go on with life and even envision a time of renewed happiness. The death of a child, a parent, a sibling, or a mate raises the stakes, and we realize that the loss took a big part of our heart and vitality.

You Have Your Own Timetable

Grieving is absolutely vital to healing and restoration. The rugged and hardy American spirit resists grief as being soft and illogical. Yet grief is inseparably connected to loving and caring. Grief helps us purge the overwhelming sense that we have lost all that is important so we can face life with all its promise and expectation. Each person grieves on his own schedule: the loss of a spouse, for example, may consume one person for years, but another person may be able to grieve even while establishing a new direction for life. (In caring for friends and families in their grief, we must not be judgmental or impose our expectations on them.) I personally tend to underestimate seriously the amount of time it takes to deal with a loss. The more the loss is intertwined with the aspirations of our hearts and lives, the longer it will take for us to come to grips with the changes and regain the balance in our lives.

> *Grieving is absolutely vital to healing and restoration . . . Grief helps us purge the overwhelming sense that we have lost all . . .*

Do Not Keep Your Grief Bottled Up

It is appropriate to share grief with those who are close to us and those directly touched by the loss. It is true that each person deals with grief in a different way, and sometimes the different ways of coping create new pain. In the poem, "Home Burial," Robert Frost tells about the way a mother and father deal with the death of an infant child. The father builds the casket and digs the grave because those practical chores provide an acceptable outlet for what he is feeling. The mother wants to talk and talk about the death of her baby, and her pain deepens because she thinks her husband doesn't feel much since he goes on with life and does not talk. Fortunately, grief can lead us to more empathetic communications and relationships, but not without effort.

> *In seasons of severe trial, the Christian has nothing on earth that he can turn to, and is therefore compelled to cast himself on his God alone.*
>
> – Charles H. Spurgeon
> *Morning and Evening*

Include God in the Painful Process

Dealing with loss requires that we draw closer to God. That is not always easy or natural, for we often feel betrayed or abandoned by God. We may even be angry with God for taking away something precious to us.

It was tremendously comforting to me when I discovered Job's speech that breaks the silence after his friends come to comfort him. Job reveals his frustration. He is angry and he challenges God. Although Job does not sin by speaking against God, he demands that God explain the loss of children, wealth, and health.

I find it very helpful to define those elements that make a loss seem unfair, seem too great a challenge, or seem inconsistent with God's plan for my life. Coming to grips with those issues over a period of time has often given me a new vision of my life and sometimes a new understanding of God. I believe that coping with loss and achieving a recovery are greatly enhanced by drawing closer to God, but I think that sometimes the closeness is achieved only after we acknowledge our "controversy" with God.

Loss always takes its toll. A person who loses a job loses self-confidence and self-esteem. A person who experiences a broken engagement feels betrayed and rejected. Those who lose a loved one know the emptiness and suffer a severe loss of direction. The nature of human life makes us all subject to loss. Yet, faith in God with His love, mercy and grace gives us the perspective to cope with that loss. The pain is there and it is genuine.

God empowers us to rediscover the joy of living. God has always had His greatest successes among those with a broken heart or a broken life.

Jesus answered, It is written: "MAN does not live on BREAD ALONE, but on every WORD that comes from the mouth of GOD." Matthew 4:4

Instead of: "I know exactly how you feel."
Try: "I can only imagine what you're going through."

Instead of: "At least he doesn't have to suffer anymore."
Try: "He suffered through a lot, didn't he?"

Instead of: "It's God's will."
Try: "One comfort I find is God's promise never to abandon us."

Instead of: "Take this pill—it will calm you down."
Try: "Do you feel like talking right now?"

Instead of: "She wouldn't want you to grieve."
Try: "It's hard to say good-bye, isn't it?"

Instead of: "Don't cry—you'll only make it worse."
Try: "Sometimes tears are the best way to express our feelings."

Instead of: "This death is a great victory for God."
Try: "Even with the promise of resurrection, it hurts to give someone up."

Instead of: "You can't be angry with God."
Try: "God understands even when we're upset."

Grieving Friend?

Instead of: "At least you have other family members."
Try: "There's no way to replace the one you've lost, is there?"

Instead of: "Don't you think it's time to get on with living your life?"
Try: "Everyone has to grieve in their own way, don't they?"

Instead of: "Don't talk about the funeral—it'll only make you sad."
Try: "We can talk about whatever you want."

Instead of: "Time heals all wounds."
Try: "Time will lessen the pain, but you'll always have a part of him/her with you."

Instead of: "You've got to be strong."
Try: "I want you to know it's okay to be yourself around me."

–Virgil Fry, Director
Lifeline Chaplaincy

Tears

by Joseph Davis

*W*hen my father died in 1979, I was devastated. My family had lived in a nice home and enjoyed many of life's luxuries, but I was now reduced to sleeping on a borrowed, portable cot. When he died, there were 52 one-dollar bills rolled up in a sock, and this was our only savings. Mom and I got by the best we could, and we eventually were "back in the black". Although we were poor, I later received a great inheritance. We had nothing, and it stands to reason that my inheritance would be proportional. It was not specified in a proper will, but it became a cherished memento, presented to me when I was 18. My inheritance was my dad's Bible. I am proud that I received what he prized most.

Recently I learned something new about my father. I was turning in my *inheritance* and reading my father's comments written in the margins. I came upon the crucifixion text, and noted something strange. He had highlighted several verses about the sufferings of Christ and in the highlighting, there were little smudges. They were tear stains.

In the 17 years I had known my father, I remembered him crying only twice. The first time was at the death of his own father, whom he absolutely worshipped. The other time, interestingly enough, was when he received this very same Bible for his 36th birthday. Dad was not the most affectionate or demonstrative man on earth. He was the one who always said things like, "Big boys don't cry" or "C'mon, be a man; tears are for wimps". Yet the emotions that he had hidden from me while alive were crying out after years in the grave. My latest find in my *inheritance* solidified my belief that what was left to me was invaluable. Although he would have never admitted it, from the grave he taught me that emotions are healthy and normal. I wish he hadn't overlooked this lesson while living.

Tears. Tiny drops of humanity that remind us that it is okay to feel. Puddles of emotion that come not only from our eyes, but from the depths of our souls to broadcast to the entire world that we are indeed human and that God's spirit is still at work within us. These shimmering pools reflect hurt, disappointment, shame, joy, sympathy, and groanings too deep for words.

I rarely cry like a baby, but I often cry like a man, and I must admit that tears have helped define me.

They have marked many of the world's greatest events. Tears of sorrow outside Lazarus's temporary tomb. Tears of sympathy at Calvary's cross. Tears of disappointment after the death of a self-proclaimed King. Tears of pain from the broken heart of Mary. Tears of shame from a disowning Peter. Tears of ecstasy peering into an empty tomb!

I rarely cry like a baby, but I often cry like a man, and I must admit that tears have helped define me. Tears of excitement while singing to my wife during our wedding. Tears of joy at the births of my two children. Tears at the funerals of friends, the victories of fellow Christians, the conversion of souls, and tears during those cherished visits to a hill called "the place of the skull".

Strength Through Sorrow

by Willard Collins

Sorrow is the strongest discipline in the world, and it gives strength and muscle to our faith. James said, "Blessed is the man who perseveres under trial, because when he has stood the test, he will receive the crown of life that God has promised to those who love Him" (James 1:12). Sorrow is the greatest schoolroom on earth.

Peter Ainslie writes,

> *They tell me I must bruise*
> *The rose's leaf*
> *Ere I can keep and use*
> *Its fragrance brief.*
>
> *They tell me love must bleed,*
> *And friendship weep,*
> *Ere in my deepest need*
> *I touch that deep.*

God shows His love for man in the chastening of His children. The author of Hebrews wrote, "And you have forgotten that word of encouragement that addresses you as sons: 'My son, do not make light of the Lord's discipline, and do not lose heart when He rebukes you, because the Lord disciplines those He loves, and He punishes everyone He accepts as a son' " (Hebrews 12:5-6).

Example of the Pine

I recently read the story of a boy and his father who hiked into the mountains. They took refuge from a storm in the shelter of great, gray boulders that lay like sleeping giants close to the crest of a lonely ridge. As the two looked upward, they saw the wind lay its mighty hands on a pine that towered from the summit of the ridge. Savagely the wind tore at it, shook it violently and howled around it.

To the boy this tree seemed about to be torn to pieces. "Look, Father," he said, pointing upward, "what the wind is doing to that pine." The full fury of the blast just then made the pine shudder and sway.

"Storms are an old story to that tree," said the father. "A tree like that lives in a struggle from the time it is high enough to catch the first breath of air. Tennyson says a tree is 'storm-strengthened on a windy site.' The strongest trees are always those that have weathered the greatest number of gales. Besides, the question is not what is happening to the tree but what is happening in the tree."

"The pine does not really seem to mind fighting the storm, does it?", the boy asked. "No, because it is able to withstand the strongest wind," the father answered. "It is the same with us. It really doesn't matter what happens *to* us but it matters a great deal what happens *in* us. You see, one's character is tested by everything that happens to him—he becomes either weaker or stronger. The test is not nearly so important as the result of the test. The old pine is safe because it resisted the first storm years and years ago and it has kept on resisting. It is getting stronger all the time. Because of what has happened in it, nothing bad can happen to it."

The same principle applies to us. Human giants have been disciplined in the schoolroom of pain, sorrow, and suffering.

Capitalize On Your Calamities

Success or failure in life will be determined on how we face our suffering. Sorrow and misfortune are not confined to any particular group. Even the apostle Paul had to endure what he called a "thorn in the flesh".

Isaiah described Christ's suffering, "He was despised and rejected by men, a man of sorrows, and familiar with suffering. Like one from whom men hide their faces, He was despised and we esteemed Him not" (Isaiah 53:3).

Misfortune can become a stepping stone to triumph. The cross of Christ, intended as a symbol of shame, has been transformed into a glorious symbol of victory.

The Best Solution

Since tribulation and trials are the expected order of life and since these experiences must come to all, the Christian must not dwell too much upon his own sorrows, but turn to assist others in bearing theirs. A person is in a mighty deplorable condition who cannot find another person in a worse condition. Christ is the best burden bearer. Since a Christian follows Christ, he is able to point others to this one who can bear their burdens. The best way to forget one's own sorrows is to lose self in the service of others.

Sorrow is the greatest schoolroom on earth.

He Is Risen – As He Said

by J. Harold Thomas

*T*he Christian has abundant reasons to believe in the resurrection of the righteous dead. If God is good and all-powerful, how could He refuse to preserve the righteous? How could He refuse to save them from the bondage and corruption of death? And God is good. And He is omnipotent.

But we have more than this perfectly logical deduction that follows from the goodness and power of God. We have a concrete, tangible, irrefutable fact. Jesus died and rose again. He gave Himself to death and allowed His body, from which all life had fled, to be laid on a cold slab in Joseph's tomb. And God vindicated the faith and assurance He had. God raised Him from the dead.

Jesus *was* raised from the dead. That is the truth of the matter.

If we believe that Jesus died and rose again, how can we doubt the resurrection of the dead? How can we doubt that those who sleep in Jesus will be brought forth again to life as he was brought again? God is good and He is all-powerful. His goodness makes him willing; His power makes Him able. And He has shown both His goodness and His power in raising His Son from the dead. In Him God abolished death and brought life and immortality to light through the gospel.

Jesus *was* raised from the dead. God brought Him forth. Therefore when Jesus comes again, "the dead in Christ will rise" (1 Thessalonians 4:16).

I KNOW THAT MY

Redeemer

LIVES

JOB 19:25

Although raised in a family that believed in God and valued Christian principles, John Newton chose to rebel against God and parents. While still a teenager, he went to work for a British slave-trading company. He worked on ships that traveled to Africa to transport slaves to the American colonies.

Conditions on the ships were horrible for the slaves where sailors were allowed to use the women to fulfill their own sexual pleasures. Newton's life and values drifted far from the teachings of his youth until one day there was a severe storm at sea which threatened the lives of all on board. Newton promised God that if He would spare his life, he would serve God the remainder of his days. His life was spared and changed by the grace of God.

John Newton later penned these words of encouragement to all who have failed to live up to their potential.

Amazing grace! How sweet the sound That saved a wretch like me! I once was lost, but now I'm found, Was blind, but now I see.

It Hurts to Lose

by Virgil Fry

*J*anet and I spoke by long-distance. It had been eight months since her 26-year-old son lost his five-year battle with cancer. He died in his dad's arms at home the weekend before Christmas. Now it was August, and she spoke of the continuing adjustments to her grief. The good days and bad days. The incredible amount of energy it took to get back to normal lifestyle functioning. She then said, "I'm learning that you can't get over this loss. You just get through it."

Losing anything precious is never easy. When something meaningful and treasured is taken from us, we grieve. It hurts to lose.

Loss and grief are not only associated with death; grief follows any significant loss. Divorce. Job layoffs. Unfulfilled dreams. Unmet expectations. Diagnosis of serious illness. Infertility or miscarriage. Relocating. Breaking or misplacing a sentimental object. Transitions in a romance or friendship. Wrecking a car. Empty nest. Financial crisis. Retirement. Any changes of personal identity or relationship.

What are the implications for people of faith? One is the incredible commonality of pain. Every time a group gathers, loss enters the gathering. People who meet in the Lord's name share the need to "bear one another's burdens". To be able to acknowledge one's pain, regardless of its origin, is to have one's burden lightened.

Some of us have learned well how to deny the pain of losing. Never let them see you sweat. Keep a stiff upper lip. Don't cry—it's a sign of weakness. I'll get through this just fine. Everything will work out.

Some of us have learned to dwell on nothing else but our losses. I'm a helpless victim of circumstance. Nobody really understands me. I don't want to get close to anyone. You could never understand how much I hurt.

Balanced between the two extremes of fierce independence and self-pitying helplessness is this message: *Life isn't fair*. The hopeful message from the Creator is: *Life is more than a few days of earthly existence*. "I have come that they may have life, and have it to the full" (John 10:10). We, life faith pilgrims, seek a "better country—a heavenly one" (Heb. 11:16).

There's more here than futuristic fantasy of the sweet bye-and-bye of heaven. There's a message of affirming, not denying, the pain of losing precious treasures. There's a message that shared tears allow emotions to be aired and deep love to flourish. There's a message that, even if we feel we've been abandoned, God is indeed with us. There's a message that the pain of losing someone precious is a barometer of how much that person, even though gone, continues to nourish us.

> *Lord, may we acknowledge our pain, feel our losses, keep our perspective that transcends the pain, and be willing to enter the pain of fellow-travelers. In the name of the One acquainted with grief. Amen.*

This I Have Learned from My Son's Death

by Glenn Martin

I have spoken words of comfort to those who have lost loved ones, but never before have their full meaning and strength been so completely impressed upon me.

Often my arm has encircled the shoulders of a bereaved one; yet, only now do I know the full solace that comes from the protective arm and sympathetic tear.

I have prayed on behalf of those who have experienced the loss of a loved one; but only now do I know fully the true consolation and blessings that come from such petitions.

I have known the love that children of God express to one another; but only now do I know more fully this love.

I have often talked of the power of the Word of God, but now I know that strength and comfort of the Bible in a new and personal encounter.

The love that God has toward His own and the price He paid in giving up His son have never before been so heart-moving to me as they are at this moment.

These lessons I have learned since the death of my son.

When Loss Is Sudden

by Pat Scott

*O*nly a few hours earlier, life was so normal. Ordinary activities were routinely accomplished without much thought. If only there were some way to turn back the clock a few short hours, perhaps something could be done to avoid an unthinkable disaster.

When we experience a sudden and irreversible loss, we feel as if some unseen attacker has blasted us into the "Twilight Zone". The blow may not have rendered us unconscious, but we are definitely dazed. At such a time, an incredible amount of activity may swirl about us, but somehow we are not a part of it. People come and go—and even talk to us. Yet, there is a sense of isolation from everyone else, as if a transparent dome had settled itself upon us. Even though we can see all the activity and may appear to be interacting, our spirit has disconnected.

One major aspect of unexpected disaster is that it does not seem real, and denial is a very tempting sedative. On the intellectual level, we know that our loved one is never coming back, but on the emotional level, we want to believe that there has been some horrible mistake. The intellect accepts the truth much sooner than the emotions can absorb it.

When the funeral is over, life is supposed to return to "normal". It is then that we may struggle with a surreal expectation that our loved one should somehow return to participate in "normal life". Those emotions are a part of our acceptance of the fact that our loss is permanent. Separating nostalgic desire from painful reality can be a wrenching exercise of will. Trying to put life in proper perspective when our little part of the world has been irreversibly damaged requires time to think and to study about God. We need at least some time to be alone to talk to God about our feelings.

Some say that their pain is so overpowering that they cannot talk to God. Satan wants us to be stuck in that rut, because in that condition we will watch helplessly as our hope withers like a plant cut off from its source of water, and we will never be who God wants us to be.

David gave praise to God for empowering him to survive a tragic period in his life. In Psalm 18:32, he said, "It is God who arms me with strength and makes my way perfect."

Overcoming the unthinkable is achieved by walking with God, for He is our source of strength. We would like to believe that we could eventually resume life with stability, security and peace—all three are found in the Lord.

Our hope need not be a hope based on wishfully thinking that no painful circumstances will befall us in this life. Rather, our hope can embody our very real expectation that God will continue to work His glorious purpose in our lives and the anticipation of a joyous reunion with the Lord and our dear loved ones.

Christ Gives Peace

by Ross W. Dye

*T*he legacy which Christ left to His people is peace. He said, "Peace I leave with you; My peace I give you. I do not give to you as the world gives. Do not let your hearts be troubled and do not be afraid" (John 14:27). The peace of which Jesus spoke here was not peace among nations, but the inner calm and quietude of spirit which comes by trusting. It is a peace born of faith that lifts the mind above the turmoil of troubled hearts. It is a peace which nothing can destroy, known only to believers. It is totally independent of incidents, reverses and troubles.

Peace Magnified with Sorrow

Many things happen in the lives of believers which make the peace of Christ more meaningful and precious in our eyes. The sorrows of life cannot destroy this peace. On the contrary, they tend to magnify this peace. The human spirit need not be imprisoned by adversity or bereavement. We may sorrow and tears may flow, but peace will never fail in Christ.

Perfect Calm in Adversity

Peace and deep spiritual joy go together. Peace is accompanied by a joy that no sorrow or trouble can undo. Paul spoke of being "sorrowful, yet always rejoicing" (2 Corinthians 6:10). There are circumstances in which it would be unnatural not to sorrow. When the heart is pierced by the arrows of tribulation, the Great Physician will heal those who trust Him. The Christian knows that no real harm can befall a saint of God, either in this world or in the world to come. All that we endure here is part of the loving discipline of a benevolent Providence and is designed for the highest good of His children. Christ was able to face adversity with such perfect calm because He was fully resigned to the will of God. When we learn to say, "Not as I will, but as You will," we shall meet our problems with serenity.

Pilgrims Here

Many view what is called an untimely death as a tragedy and any death as a calamity, but this is only from our human point of view. Paul said, "To die is gain" (Philippians 1:21). He knew it is far better to depart and be with Christ. It is natural, however, for us to weep when earth's ties are broken. It is not wrong to weep, but our hope in Christ keeps our sorrow from destroying our peace. To the spiritual person, troubles are viewed as a part of a rapidly changing scene which will soon usher in an eternal day of joy even as the light follows the darkness. The transiency of all things earthly encourages the heart to fix its affections upon the things which are above. We are pilgrims in this present world, and we know we have no permanency here. We look up in hope and see that Christ is leading us home.

The Unseen Becomes Real

Bereavement can deepen the believer's peace, for it makes the unseen more real and quickens our awareness of immortality. I have never felt so great kinship with Christ, nor have I been so keenly aware of the source of my peace as when immersed in heart-rending sorrow. Peace is a condition of heart in which the believer trusts when he cannot see and believes when he cannot understand.

Peace is our heritage as Christ's people. If we do not know this peace, we do not know the Prince of Peace as we ought.

Joy and peace come from believing. They describe different aspects of the believer's happiness. Peace may be represented by a placid stream, and joy by the singing of a rapid fountain. One represents faith in action; the other suggests faith at rest in God. The gospel is a remedy for present ills and a foretaste of coming bliss; it is designed to transform the life, restore the soul and rejoice the heart in hope. As we appreciate these blessings, they can become personal realities. It is my prayer that "the God of hope fill you with all joy and peace as you trust in Him, so that you may overflow with hope by the power of the Holy Spirit" (Romans 15:13).

Peace, Perfect Peace

"You will keep in perfect peace Him whose mind is steadfast, because He trusts in you" (Isaiah 26:3).

Peace, perfect peace, in this dark world of sin:
The blood of Jesus whispers "peace" within.

Peace, perfect peace, by thronging duties pressed;
To do the will of Jesus—this is rest.

Peace, perfect peace, with sorrows surging round:
On Jesus' bosom naught but calm is found.

Peace, perfect peace, our future all unknown:
Jesus we know, and He is on the throne.

Peace, perfect peace, Death shadowing us and ours:
Jesus has vanquished Death and all its powers.

It is enough; earth's struggles soon shall cease,
And Jesus call us to heav'n's perfect peace.

—Edward H. Bickersteth

Prayer Has Power

by Frank L. Cox

*T*he great forces of the universe are the silent forces such as gravity or light. It is also true of prayer. Though unseen, it is one of the mightiest weapons that the Almighty God has placed in the hand of man.

Pardoning Power

All men stand in need of divine pardon: for "there is none righteous, no, not one"; "for all have sinned, and fall short of the glory of God." We sin through ignorance, through weakness, through presumption, through neglect of sacred duty. There are sins of the body, and there are sins of the disposition. And without pardon from above, there is no salvation. But a humble petition from the penitent child of God reaches the throne of mercy, touches the Father's heart and secures abundant pardon. "Let the wicked forsake his way and the evil man his thoughts. Let him turn to the Lord, and He will have mercy on him, and to our God, for He will freely pardon" (Isaiah 55:7). The Savior taught the disciples to pray: "And forgive us our debts, as we also have forgiven our debtors."

> *You are, to me, an amazingly cheerful God, And I pray that some day I shall learn Your secret.*
>
> – M. Scott Peck
> *The Road Less Traveled and Beyond*

39

Enlightening Power

Though we may have knowledge, we do not always know how to apply it, how to solve the intricate problem, how to act when the crisis comes. When Solomon as a youthful king prayed for "an understanding heart," his petition was granted. A New Testament writer says: "If any of you lacks wisdom, he should ask God, who gives generously to all without finding fault, and it will be given him" (James 1:5,6). Prayerful people become wise people. Men who pray out of a pure heart are saved from the embarrassment of their own folly.

Comforting Power

Divine comfort is greatly needed. Hearts are broken, bowed down with sorrow, filled with fear. Anxiety, bereavement, and temptation beset us. A humble prayer to "the God of all comfort" brings relief, binds up the broken heart, lightens the burden. Through prayer, Jesus found relief and obtained strength to face the foe. The apostle Paul prayed: "May our Lord Jesus Christ Himself and God our Father, who loved us and by His grace gave us eternal encouragement and good hope, encourage your hearts and strengthen you in every good deed and word " (2 Thessalonians 2:16,17). Is your heart heavy? Look to God in prayer.

> *The lesson that the Lord taught me—and is still teaching me—is that He is the one who controls the peace that I crave.*
>
> –Gary Pierce
> *Beyond the Storm*

I CAN DO **EVERYTHING** THROUGH **HIM** WHO GIVES ME **STRENGTH**

PHILIPPIANS 4:13

Enriching Power

How empty our lives! How void of God! How unlike the Christ, our pattern! With all our attainments and our accomplishments and our accumulations, we are paupers! But God enriches our lives when we ask Him in fullness of faith. As God sent Elijah rain in answer to prayer, will He not send us showers of blessings if we humbly ask Him? Not necessarily what we desire, but what we need He gives. And Jesus said: "Ask and it will be given you; seek and you will find; knock and the door will be opened to you. For every one who asks receives; and he who seeks finds; and to him who knocks, the door will be opened" (Matthew 7:7, 8).

The power of prayer! A power that brings pardon, that enlightens, that comforts, that transforms, that enriches! Prayer is powerful because it lays hold on the Source of Power. Prayer is often great unused power! Maclaren said, "If man is admitted into the bullion vault, and comes out empty handed, whose fault is it he is poor?" Let us pray earnestly and continually for God's blessings through prayer.

Bitter or Better?

by Bill McDonald

Toward the end of his life, Solomon contemplated life's mysteries, trials, and injustices. His ultimate answer to life's tough questions was, "Fear God and keep His commandments, for this is the whole duty of man" (Ecclesiastes 12:13). Our journey through grief presents many of the same mysteries and trials. We long for answers to our questions and an end to the pain which has taken up residence in our lives.

The process of grief leads us to a very basic conclusion. Grief will either make us bitter or make us better. The outcome seems to be a mystery to those in the grip of grief. Grief can leave us withdrawn, isolated, and with a loss of ability to love, feel, or even care. For others the process of grief creates a deeper sense of caring and love.

Research by Bill Bates through his *Life Appreciation Training* indicates that we can be in charge of the outcome of grief. He has identified six characteristics of people who successfully navigate the straits of grief.

Successful grievers find someone who will share their pain.

They find people who will listen with compassionate ears and provide a safety net for them to explore their feelings and fears. Talking with someone who cares serves as a cleansing agent for pain, anger, and fear. We were not designed to go through the grief process alone. We need a friend to go through it with us. James 5:16 could be paraphrased for the grief-stricken, "Share your struggles with one another and pray for one another that you may be healed."

Better grievers make conscious decisions to move forward.

They recognize the pain of this day and are willing to move forward toward better days. Many people choose to stay in their grief for a variety of reasons. Some stay there trying to show the depth of their love for the deceased. Others simply choose the predictability of the pain of grief rather than risks of new responsibilities alone. Those who grieve successfully find ways to let go of the past and move forward with their lives. "Forgetting what is behind and straining toward what is ahead, I press on toward the goal..." (Philippians 3:13,14).

Before any beginning can take place, an ending must be realized. We cannot journey forward until we accept the loss that has occurred.

Successful grievers clean up relationships.

They learn to make amends for their past mistakes and to become forgivers of the mistakes of others. They have discovered the heaviness of the burdens of anger, guilt, and hurt. They have learned that life is hard enough without carrying unnecessary burdens.

Those who successfully negotiate grief know that happiness and bitterness cannot live peacefully in the same heart.

43

If a brother has offended them, they make every effort to find a peaceful resolution. If they have hurt someone else, they go seeking forgiveness.

Better grievers learn the simple, but profound lesson: What you give is what you get.

Life tends to be very reciprocal in nature. What you give tends to come back to you. Therefore, if you need compassion, you should show compassion. If you long for hope, you should give hope to others. If you want to be loved, you must show love to others. When we do the right things for others, they tend to do the right things for us. This simple truth is at the heart of the Golden Rule.

> O Joy that seekest me thro' pain, I cannot close my heart to Thee. I trace the rainbow thro' the rain. And feel the promise is not in vain, That morn shall tearless be.
>
> – George Matheson
> *O Love That Will Not Let Me Go*

Better grievers learn to live in the present moment.

They take life's gifts and pleasures and give themselves permission to enjoy them right now. They realize that nothing about yesterday can be changed or undone. Tomorrow's arrival is not guaranteed. This present moment is all that you have. Time spent in yesterdays and tomorrows is wasted and does not lead to successful grieving. You must do your best with this 24-hour package called "today."

Successful grievers find ways to share what they've learned with others.

No one can help you through the pain better than someone who has experienced it. As you learn to cope with your losses, be willing to share what you've learned with others. You have traveled the peaks and valleys. You have experienced the good days as well as the days when memories crippled your ability to function normally. As a survivor of life's toughest test, share what you've learned. Let others know that they will laugh again, love again, give again, hope again. Help someone else carry their load of grief. Comfort cannot be hoarded. God's comfort equips us to comfort others along the way (2 Corinthians 1:3,4).

To have setbacks in the grieving process is perfectly normal, but to get stuck in the process is the road to bitterness. If you are just beginning the grieving process, remember that grief is like a tunnel. You enter the darkness of despair from a life that is forever changed. You must now journey through the darkness to a new life— different from the former, but one as beautiful as you determine to let it be. Bitter or better? The choice is yours.

To successfully grieve means that we have become better people, who, with a sense of choice, have faced life with its heartache and learned to live again.

Reunion In Heaven

by R. C. Bell

*U*ntil death man comprises "spirit, soul and body" (1 Thessalonians 5:23). After death he lives on conscious and aware, without his body until he gets it back, raised from the dead, that he may be a complete man again. A Christian man between death and resurrection, though unbodied, is "with Christ," enjoying a "far better" life than he knew before his death (Philippians 1:23).

Christ Recognizable

What change did Christ's death and resurrection make in Him? In personality, none. He was still the same person, still loved by the same friends and still hated by the same foes. And His body, though a strange change had taken place in the nature of its substance, was unchanged in form.

Death is real, but it is not the destiny for which we were created and the grave is not the goal.

– Robert Shank

In His risen body, Christ repeatedly appeared to His disciples. They saw, heard, and handled Him. They walked, talked, and ate with Him. They knew Him to be the same man, unaltered in personality and bodily appearance.

Christ the Firstfruits

"But Christ has indeed been raised from the dead, the firstfruits of those who have fallen" (I Corinthians 15:20). As evidence and sample of the harvest that was beginning,

Jews "offered" the fruit gathered first to God. This verse teaches that Christ's resurrection is evidence and example of the resurrection His saints may expect at His coming. Another scripture that teaches the same thing reads simply: "We know that when He appears, we shall be like Him" (I John 3:2). The birth, death, and resurrection of Christ are not exceptionable; they are the common lot of all men.

That a natural body asleep in Jesus shall be awakened, with its identity preserved, still a body but a spiritual body, "conformed to His glorious body" (Philippians 3:21) and recognizable as His was, is a conclusion unavoidable. "It is sown a natural body... If there is a natural body, there is also a spiritual body" (I Corinthians 15:44). A spiritual resurrection-body is as certain and as actual as a natural body. A person without a body may be an angel, but certainly not a man as God made him, and as he shall be again when his redemption is perfected. If by altering its atomic structure man can change matter into energy, why is it incredible that God the Maker of man and matter, can, without changing its form, turn a natural body into a spiritual body? Is this more wonderful than making our natural body to begin with, out of dust?

Reunion

Some seem to think that in heaven saints will sit on clouds and play harps for all eternity. Insofar as the Bible paints celestial scenery and life, it uses colors taken from the palette of terrestrial life. And the pictures minister to our natural and proper longing for a human heaven.

Christ's story of the rich man and Lazarus teaches that memory and natural affection survive death. The rich man in Hades is still concerned about his brothers yet alive on earth (Luke 16:28). How we love even the very bodies of our close kin. Instead of being lost to us forever at death, their bodies together with ours, incapable of weariness, suffering, deformity, and death, shall be raised that the whole triune man, "spirit, soul and body" may "be kept blameless at the coming of our Lord Jesus Christ" (I Thessalonians 5:23).

Sing to Me of Heaven

Sing to me of heaven, sing that song of peace,
From the toils that bind me it will bring release;
Burdens will be lifted that are pressing so,
Showers of great blessing o'er my heart will flow.

Sing to me of heaven, as I walk alone,
Dreaming of the comrades that so long have gone;
In a fairer region 'mong the angel throng,
They are happy as they sing that old, sweet song.

Sing to me of heaven, tenderly and low,
Till the shadows o'er me rise and swiftly go;
When my heart is weary, when the day is long,
Sing to me of heaven, sing that old, sweet song.

Refrain:
Sing to me of heaven, let me fondly dream
Of its golden glory, of its pearly gleam;
Sing to me when shadows of the evening fall,
Sing to me of heaven, Sweetest song of all.

Comfort from God's Word

*I*magine how lost you would feel on a long trip without a map. With that image, you would get a sense of the hopelessness of the journey through grief without God's Word for guidance. When the path is dark, His Word is light. When our way is threatening, His Word provides security. When our courage is diminished, His Word gives confidence.

The Bible tells the whole truth about its heroes. It records their triumphs as well as their dark moments of doubt and despair. In those real people we find the hope to continue with our lives. Go with Mary and Martha to the tomb of their brother, Lazarus. Weep with David over the loss of his infant son. Catch a glimpse of John's heavenly vision of a world restored to its original order. The Bible reminds us that although we have lost a loved one, God is still our constant companion and guide. He has promised that He would never leave us or forsake us—and He can be trusted to keep His promises.

Do more than read the words of comfort from Scripture. Meditate on them. Pray with these words in your heart. Place your trust and confidence in the One who inspired them. They are a solid rock in your shaken world.

Ps 6:2-9

2   Be merciful to me, LORD, for I am faint; O LORD, heal me, for my bones are in agony.

3   My soul is in anguish. How long, O LORD, how long?

4   Turn, O LORD, and deliver me; save me because of Your unfailing love.

5   No one remembers you when he is dead. Who praises You from the grave?

6   I am worn out from groaning; all night long I flood my bed with weeping and drench my couch with tears.

7   My eyes grow weak with sorrow; they fail because of all my foes.

8   Away from me, all you who do evil, for the LORD has heard my weeping.

9   The LORD has heard my cry for mercy; the LORD accepts my prayer.

Ps 55:22

22 Cast your cares on the LORD and He will sustain you; He will never let the righteous fall.

Heb 4:14-16

14 Therefore, since we have a great high priest who has gone through the heavens, Jesus the Son of God, let us hold firmly to the faith we profess.

15 For we do not have a high priest who is unable to sympathize with our weaknesses, but we have one who has been tempted in every way, just as we are—yet was without sin.

16 Let us then approach the throne of grace with confidence, so that we may receive mercy and find grace to help us in our time of need.

John 14:1-3

1 "Do not let your hearts be troubled. Trust in God; trust also in Me.

2 In My Father's house are many rooms; if it were not so, I would have told you. I am going there to prepare a place for you.

3 And if I go and prepare a place for you, I will come back and take you to be with Me that you also may be where I am.

II Th 2:16

16 May our Lord Jesus Christ himself and God our Father, who loved us and by His grace gave us eternal encouragement and good hope...

Col 3:1

1   Since, then, you have been raised with Christ, set
    your hearts on things above, where Christ is seated
    at the right hand of God.

Isa 48:17

17 This is what the LORD says—your Redeemer, the
    Holy One of Israel: "I am the LORD your God, who
    teaches you what is best for you, who directs you in
    the way you should go."

John 14:27

27 Peace I leave with you; My peace I give you. I do not
    give to you as the world gives. Do not let your hearts
    be troubled and do not be afraid.

2 Cor 1:3-4

3   Praise be to the God and Father of our Lord Jesus
    Christ, the Father of compassion and the God of all
    comfort,

4   who comforts us in all our troubles, so that we can
    comfort those in any trouble with the comfort we
    ourselves have received from God.

Rev 7:17

17 "For the Lamb at the center of the throne will be their shepherd; He will lead them to springs of living water. And God will wipe away every tear from their eyes."

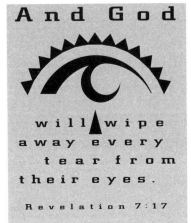

Isa 66:13

13 "As a mother comforts her child, so will I comfort you; and you will be comforted over Jerusalem."

Zeph 3:17

17 The LORD your God is with you, He is mighty to save. He will take great delight in you, He will quiet you with His love, He will rejoice over you with singing."

Ps 116:15

15 Precious in the sight of the LORD is the death of His saints.

Ps 42:1-6

1 As the deer pants for streams of water, so my soul pants for You, O God.

2 My soul thirsts for God, for the living God. When can I go and meet with God?

3 My tears have been my food day and night, while men say to me all day long, "Where is your God?"

4 These things I remember as I pour out my soul: how I used to go with the multitude, leading the procession to the house of God, with shouts of joy and thanksgiving among the festive throng.

5 Why are you downcast, O my soul? Why so disturbed within me? Put your hope in God, for I will yet praise Him, my Savior and

6 my God. My soul is downcast within me; therefore I will remember You from the land of the Jordan, the heights of Hermon—from Mount Mizar.

2 Sam 12:18-23

18 On the seventh day the child died. David's servants were afraid to tell him that the child was dead, for they thought, "While the child was still living, we spoke to David but he would not listen to us. How can we tell him the child is dead? He may do something desperate."

19 David noticed that his servants were whispering among themselves and he realized the child was dead. "Is the child dead?" he asked. "Yes," they replied, "he is dead."

20 Then David got up from the ground. After he had washed, put on lotions and changed his clothes, he went into the house of the LORD and worshiped. Then he went to his own house, and at his request they served him food, and he ate.

21 His servants asked him, "Why are you acting this way? While the child was alive, you fasted and wept, but now that the child is dead, you get up and eat!"

22 He answered, "While the child was still alive, I fasted and wept. I thought, 'Who knows? The LORD may be gracious to me and let the child live.'

23 But now that he is dead, why should I fast? Can I bring him back again? I will go to him, but he will not return to me."

Matt 5:4

4   Blessed are those who mourn, for they will be comforted.

Matt 11:29-30

29 "Take My yoke upon you and learn from Me, for I am gentle and humble in heart, and you will find rest for your souls.

30 For My yoke is easy and My burden is light."

"Come to Me, all you who are weary and burdened, and I will give you rest."

Matthew 11:28

John 11:17-44

17 On his arrival, Jesus found that Lazarus had already been in the tomb for four days.

18 Bethany was less than two miles from Jerusalem,

19 and many Jews had come to Martha and Mary to comfort them in the loss of their brother.

20 When Martha heard that Jesus was coming, she went out to meet Him, but Mary stayed at home.

21 "Lord," Martha said to Jesus, "if You had been here, my brother would not have died.

22 But I know that even now God will give You whatever You ask."

23 Jesus said to her, "Your brother will rise again."

24 Martha answered, "I know he will rise again in the resurrection at the last day."

25 Jesus said to her, "I am the resurrection and the life. He who believes in Me will live, even though he dies;

26 and whoever lives and believes in Me will never die. Do you believe this?"

27 "Yes, Lord," she told Him, "I believe that You are the Christ, the Son of God, who was to come into the world."

28 And after she had said this, she went back and called her sister Mary aside. "The Teacher is here," she said, "and is asking for you."

29 When Mary heard this, she got up quickly and went to Him.

30 Now Jesus had not yet entered the village, but was still at the place where Martha had met Him.

31 When the Jews who had been with Mary in the house, comforting her, noticed how quickly she got up and went out, they followed her, supposing she was going to the tomb to mourn there.

32 When Mary reached the place where Jesus was and saw Him, she fell at his feet and said, "Lord, if You had been here, my brother would not have died."

33 When Jesus saw her weeping, and the Jews who had come along with her also weeping, He was deeply moved in spirit and troubled.

34 "Where have you laid him?" he asked. "Come and see, Lord," they replied.

35 Jesus wept.

36 Then the Jews said, "See how He loved him!"

37 But some of them said, "Could not he who opened the eyes of the blind man have kept this man from dying?"

38 Jesus, once more deeply moved, came to the tomb. It was a cave with a stone laid across the entrance.

39 "Take away the stone," he said. "But, Lord," said Martha, the sister of the dead man, "by this time there is a bad odor, for he has been there four days."

40 Then Jesus said, "Did I not tell you that if you believed, you would see the glory of God?"

41 So they took away the stone. Then Jesus looked up and said, "Father, I thank You that You have heard Me.

42 I knew that you always hear Me, but I said this for the benefit of the people standing here, that they may believe that You sent Me."

43 When He had said this, Jesus called in a loud voice, "Lazarus, come out!"

44 The dead man came out, his hands and feet wrapped with strips of linen, and a cloth around his face. Jesus said to them, "Take off the grave clothes and let him go."

NO ONE
COMES TO THE
FATHER,

BUT
BY
ME.

JOHN 14:6

John 14:1-4

1 "Do not let your hearts be troubled. Trust in God; trust also in Me.

2 In My Father's house are many rooms; if it were not so, I would have told you. I am going there to prepare a place for you.

3 And if I go and prepare a place for you, I will come back and take you to be with Me that you also may be where I am.

4 You know the way to the place where I am going."

Rom 8:35-39

35 Who shall separate us from the love of Christ? Shall trouble or hardship or persecution or famine or nakedness or danger or sword?

36 As it is written: "For your sake we face death all day long; we are considered as sheep to be slaughtered."

37 No, in all these things we are more than conquerors through Him who loved us.

38 For I am convinced that neither death nor life, neither angels nor demons, neither the present nor the future, nor any powers,

39 neither height nor depth, nor anything else in all creation, will be able to separate us from the love of God that is in Christ Jesus our Lord.

1 Cor 10:13

13 No temptation has seized you except what is common to man. And God is faithful; He will not let you be tempted beyond what you can bear. But when you are tempted, He will also provide a way out so that you can stand up under it.

1 Cor 15:35-57

35 But someone may ask, "How are the dead raised? With what kind of body will they come?"

36 How foolish! What you sow does not come to life unless it dies.

37 When you sow, you do not plant the body that will be, but just a seed, perhaps of wheat or of something else.

38 But God gives it a body as He has determined, and to each kind of seed He gives its own body.

39 All flesh is not the same: Men have one kind of flesh, animals have another, birds another and fish another.

40 There are also heavenly bodies and there are earthly bodies; but the splendor of the heavenly bodies is one kind, and the splendor of the earthly bodies is another.

41 The sun has one kind of splendor, the moon another and the stars another; and star differs from star in splendor.

42 So will it be with the resurrection of the dead. The body that is sown is perishable, it is raised imperishable;

43 it is sown in dishonor, it is raised in glory; it is sown in weakness, it is raised in power;

44 it is sown a natural body, it is raised a spiritual body. If there is a natural body, there is also a spiritual body.

45 So it is written: "The first man Adam became a living being"; the last Adam, a life-giving spirit.

46 The spiritual did not come first, but the natural, and after that the spiritual.

47 The first man was of the dust of the earth, the second man from heaven.

48 As was the earthly man, so are those who are of the earth; and as is the man from heaven, so also are those who are of heaven.

49 And just as we have borne the likeness of the earthly man, so shall we bear the likeness of the man from heaven.

50 I declare to you, brothers, that flesh and blood cannot inherit the kingdom of God, nor does the perishable inherit the imperishable.

51 Listen, I tell you a mystery: We will not all sleep, but we will all be changed—

52 in a flash, in the twinkling of an eye, at the last trumpet. For the trumpet will sound, the dead will be raised imperishable, and we will be changed.

53 For the perishable must clothe itself with the imperishable, and the mortal with immortality.

54 When the perishable has been clothed with the
imperishable, and the mortal with immortality, then
the saying that is written will come true: "Death has
been swallowed up in victory."

55 "Where, O death, is your victory? Where, O death,
is your sting?"

56 The sting of death is sin, and the power of sin is
the law.

57 But thanks be to God! He gives us the victory
through our Lord Jesus Christ.

2 Cor 1:3-4

3 Praise be to the God
and Father of our Lord
Jesus Christ, the Father
of compassion and the
God of all comfort,

4 who comforts us in all
our troubles, so that we
can comfort those in
any trouble with the
comfort we ourselves
have received from
God.

But Seek First
His Kingdom
& His Righteousness,
and all these things will
be given to you as well.
Matthew 6:33

2 Cor 5:1-8

1 Now we know that if the earthly tent we live in is destroyed, we have a building from God, an eternal house in heaven, not built by human hands.

2 Meanwhile we groan, longing to be clothed with our heavenly dwelling,

3 because when we are clothed, we will not be found naked.

4 For while we are in this tent, we groan and are burdened, because we do not wish to be unclothed but to be clothed with our heavenly dwelling, so that what is mortal may be swallowed up by life.

5 Now it is God who has made us for this very purpose and has given us the Spirit as a deposit, guaranteeing what is to come.

6 Therefore we are always confident and know that as long as we are at home in the body we are away from the Lord.

7 We live by faith, not by sight.

8 We are confident, I say, and would prefer to be away from the body and at home with the Lord.

BLESSED *is the man who does not walk in the counsel of the wicked...*

Psalm 1:1

About Some of the Authors

The late **M. Norvel Young** dedicated his life to Christian education at the university level. His positive outlook on life blessed countless thousands around the world as he completed more than forty international trips. Young studied the lives of those who had achieved special success in the 20th Century and shared their insights in the book, *Living Lights, Shining Stars*. His own fascinating life story is told in *Forever Young* by Bill Henegar and Jerry Rushford.

Helen M. Young is a nationally known writer and speaker, mother of four children, and wife of the late M. Norvel Young. Her gracious insight and encouraging vision have inspired women for decades. She has written for and edited Christian publications and authored a timeless booklet entitled *Children Won't Wait*. She co-authored *Time Management for Christian Women* which offers sound advice to modern women. The passing of her husband especially equipped her to share her heart on bereavement.

Virgil Fry heads up the Lifeline Chaplaincy of M.D. Anderson Hospital in Houston, Texas. His daily contact with those who are grieving the loss of loved ones to cancer shows in the deep sensitivity and insight of his writing. Fry edits a newsletter for this prestigious hospital and has distilled his experience in his book, *Disrupted*.

Joseph Davis shares with his readers from life experience, including the death of his father. As a youth minister and preacher, Davis has walked by the side of many who were going through times of grief. He shares more than fifty stories of God's incredible work in ordinary lives in his book, *Water to Wine*.

Willard Collins is one of the most powerful and successful evangelists of his day. He is an expert at wedding the gospel truth with pure human emotion that has moved thousands to obey the call of Jesus. As an administrator of a Christian college, he commanded the love and respect of students and faculty. He lives on today as one of the most respected voices for the cause of Jesus Christ and his life story is told in the book, *Willard Collins: The People Person.*

Randy Becton, a cancer survivor himself, gives hope and strength to those dealing with the devastation of cancer. He is a nationally known speaker on a weekly syndicated religious television program and frequently makes guest appearances on talk-radio programs. He is the author of *Everyday Strength, Everyday Evangelism,* and *Everyday Comfort* and the director of Caring Cancer Ministry.

Pat Scott was suddenly widowed when an armed robber shot and killed her husband in the driveway of their Dallas home as she helplessly watched. She tells the story of her personal passage through grief in the book, *Batten Down the Hatches.* She has continued to live her life in service to the Lord's church at her local congregation and as a speaker across the country.

Bill McDonald helps families through the grief process through Grief Recovery Workshops offered around the country. McDonald is a leader in his local congregation as well as the owner of a highly-respected funeral home in his community. His deep compassion for the bereaved is an asset to both church and community.

And Now What About You?

As you make your way through the grief process, many questions remain unanswered. But perhaps the most important question you can ask right now is, "What about me?" You have given yourself for your departed loved one. What now? What's next? Where do you go from here?

First and foremost, your future happiness is to be found with God. Life without Him is empty and meaningless. Life with God is rich and full, both in this life and for eternity. Eternity with God means never experiencing pain, sorrow, or loss again.

Your past sorrows and grief cannot be erased in this life, but your future can be secured by the choices you make now. Turn to God and let Him comfort you. Learn of God and see that He is worthy to be praised and followed. Love God with all your heart, mind, and strength and begin experiencing His blessings in this life as you make wise preparation for the life to come.

Choose God; He's already chosen you.

Your Thoughts

Your Thoughts

Your Thoughts

Look Great.
Feel Great.
& Still Eat Pizza!

You don't have to be a health freak to be healthy, it's easier than you think

Jason Cerniglia
Owner, Hoover Fitness

Preventative Health Specialist

Disclaimer

The information in this book is intended to be applied to your diet and exercise in a safe and appropriate manner. Jason Cerniglia, Hoover Fitness L.L.C, and all other affiliates in no way claim responsibility or guarantee any specific results or specific health improvements. Jason Cerniglia, Hoover Fitness L.L.C., and all other affiliates do not attempt to diagnose or treat any health problems. Jason Cerniglia, Hoover Fitness L.L.C., and all other affiliates urge you to consult a doctor before changing your diet and before starting any new exercise routines. Jason Cerniglia, Hoover Fitness L.L.C., and all affiliates hold no responsibility to your health as a result of reading this book. DIET AND EXERCISE AT YOUR OWN RISK. *WORK HARD, BUT WORK SAFE.*

Table of Contents

I. ABOUT THE AUTHOR

Jason Cerniglia is a certified personal trainer, certified sports nutritionist, certified golf conditioning coach, and a veteran of the fitness industry for over ten years. He is the owner of Hoover Fitness, JC Personal Training, Hoover Fitness Consulting, Strength Through Faith Charity, and a few other health-related businesses. Jason was born and raised in Hoover, Alabama, attended High School at W.A. Berry in Hoover, and graduated from Auburn University. He has spent his entire life training and developing his body and mind through the principles listed in this book. Jason has spent the last ten years working with hundreds of clients on diet and exercise, and for the past three years as an owner of a health club. In July of 2008, Jason was named by *Club Solutions Magazine* as the "Most Fit Health Club Professional in America." Jason is now actively involved in the "preventative health movement" in America, and his goal is to make a tremendous impact on helping America improve its physical and economic problems caused by obesity and other preventative health problems. He is a fitness professional and a preventative health specialist.

II. INTRODUCTION

Everyone wants to look better, feel better, and be healthier. If you didn't, you wouldn't have this book in your hands. Improved health and fitness is a lifestyle. It is a habit. It has to be part of your life. But…it doesn't have to be all *that* bad. You don't have to starve yourself or eat foods that you don't like. You don't have to exercise everyday until you pass out. You just have to make exercise and eating better a part of your life. You have to make it a habit.

In this book, you will learn a progressive approach to improved health and wellness. You will also learn the mental approach to diet and exercise, and how to take control of your situation by making better choices and avoiding failure situations.

Your "situation" is your diet and exercise. I have spent a lifetime working on my situation and my entire adult life working on other people's situations. I am not a doctor, although I probably get more medical questions than a doctor. I am not a physical therapist. I am not a registered dietician. I am, however, a fitness professional. I am a personal trainer, a sports nutritionist, a golf conditioning coach, and a health club owner. I am what I consider a preventative health specialist or a wellness coach. I can't prescribe medicine or perform surgery or physical therapy, but what I can do is provide you with the tools needed to *decrease* your chances having to take medicine or needing surgery or physical therapy. I can show you how to become a healthier you. If you apply the principles of this book, you will look better, feel better, and drastically improve your health.

Over the past several years, we have become lazy and learned to rely on medications and treatments to bail us out of whatever situation we find ourselves. This "easy" system has created a health and economic nightmare. Applying the information learned in this book will help *prevent* problems as opposed to having to *treat* problems. If more people start taking a proactive approach, our health and economic problems will improve. Oh yeah, and if you apply the information that you learn by reading this book, you will also look better, sleep better, feel better, and still get to eat pizza and eat ice cream!

There are a lot of right and wrong ways to exercise and diet. I will show you what I think are some of the right ways. These aren't the only ways, but they are ways that I know *can* be effective. Take any information from this book that can help improve your situation and apply it. You *will* see results if you make improvements to your diet and exercise.

III.
TAKE CONTROL OF *YOUR* HEALTH

CHAPTER ONE

Preventative Health – A Proactive Approach

According to recent statistics, two thirds of Americans are overweight and one third is considered obese. Americans have become lazy and basically have stopped taking care of themselves. Only 14 percent of Americans belong to a health club, and we all know that not everyone who belongs to a health club uses it. So, in reality, only about 10 percent of our population exercises in a health club. What does all this mean? It means that we are a very overweight society, and the health problems are starting to add up—physically and financially.

The financial toll on our country due to disease and health care costs is enormous. Our health care system is a nightmare. People keep getting sick and relying on insurance to pay for all of their treatments. Our health care system is actually a "sick care" system. We have to move toward prevention and away from treatment. Health insurance needs to be exactly what it is, insurance. The premise of any insurance is the same. Insurance is there to bail you out when a catastrophe occurs. Insurance is not meant to be there to pay a $500 doctor visit or for medicine every time you sneeze, cough, or have a stomach ache. Obesity, which is preventable, is accountable for nearly one third of our health care costs! Each week, 1.2 million Americans visit emergency rooms for non-accident related problems—basically, for problems that could have been prevented. If people would take better care of themselves, they would not have to rely on their insurance as much. Insurance would not have to be used for the problems that could have been prevented. Insurance would be used for what it is supposed to be used for—to help you in a tragic, unpreventable situation. People need to become non-dependent on health insurance. I am not saying that we shouldn't have insurance or that you should never go to the doctor. What I am saying is that if we take better care of ourselves, we will visit the doctor less often and use our insurance less often, and save ourselves, the government, insurance companies, and the entire population a great amount of money; *and* we will feel better and look better at the same time. Like everything else, health insurance can be abused if given the chance. Be smart and get proactive with your health.

You can actually make money by being healthier.

The government, health care companies, and large and small business would all save billions of dollars if people would just take better care of themselves. That would also lead to a huge economic boost that would trickle down to the average person for their benefit. You, as an individual, can also benefit directly. Less sick days, more productivity at work, fewer co-pays for doctor visits, and so on. These things can add up.

Treatment is an easier sell than prevention.

We need to reverse our thinking from "treating" to "preventing." Treatment is an easier sell than prevention. It's easy not to take care of yourself, get sick, go to the doctor and get some medicine, then fix the problem. That requires no hard work. It actually takes some work to be proactive and work toward preventing problems instead of treating them. It seems hard at first and you might be thinking, "I am ok the way I do things now" or "I have no reason to take better care of myself, things are good now, why would I want to work for this." Chances are that you aren't happy with the way you look and feel, but even if you are ok with it, you need to work toward preventing the "big one." As stated before, we are facing two major problems: minor illnesses are too common and people are not taking measures to reduce their chances of serious or life-threatening illnesses. There are major health problems that can be prevented. Type 2 diabetes, coronary heart disease, and certain types of cancer can all be prevented by taking better care of yourself. Also, metabolic syndrome, sleep apnea, osteoarthritis, gallbladder disease, liver disease, pregnancy complications, and osteoporosis can be prevented as a result of diet and exercise. I am not saying that you will never get sick or acquire a disease, but what I am saying, and what thousands of studies have determined, is that if you improve your diet and exercise, you will look better, feel better, get sick less, and decrease your chances of having major health problems or disease. If everyone would make these lifestyle improvements, the improvements in our society and economy would be tremendous. We can't change everyone, but if we all make changes, with ourselves, the rest will fall into place.

"I can't afford a gym membership."
"I don't have time to exercise."

If you really can't afford a gym membership, then get outside and run or walk. Do some exercises at your home. Find something to do. Although, chances are you really can afford $35 per month to join a health club. People pay for the things that are important to them. As for not having time to exercise, people make time for the things that are important to them. You may have to get creative. Things may be inconvenient at first, but things will get easier. Time and economic reasons for not exercising are just barriers you created. You have to eliminate these barriers. They are just a way of hiding from the truth. Everyone knows that they should take better care of themselves. Stop making excuses and start today. You will not see immediate effects, but look at the big picture and see all the good that *will* take place. Do it for yourself. Do it for your spouse. Do it for your kids. Whatever the reason needs to be, just take better care of yourself. Change your thinking. Think *prevent*, not *treat*.

CHAPTER TWO

Control Your Mind – Avoid Mental Mistakes

Too often, people get a workout plan or diet plan and try to follow it precisely; then they get frustrated and quit. They don't think about the plan; they just do it. This leads them to failure. They create excuses for why not, instead of why. They put themselves in situations that hinder their progress. Mentally, people take the wrong approach to exercise and diet and it assists them in failure. I have spent many years working on the mental side of exercise and diet, learning to get control of my head. If you take certain mental approaches to diet and exercise, it will be easier to achieve your goals. Later chapters in this book will discuss diet and exercise specifics, but before we get to any of that, we must attack the mental side of diet and exercise.

Change your thinking first.

Your first step to diet and exercise does not require any diet or any exercise. It requires that you change your thinking. Change your mental approach. If you can get control of your head, you will be able to diet better and exercise more. Apply these mental changes to the diet and exercise that you learn in this book and you *will* see results.

You don't have to be a fitness fanatic to get results.

Work hard enough to keep going, but not so hard that you quit. You have to create a balance. You have to be happy. You can get in better shape and achieve all the results in the world, and still be happy. You don't have to be a fitness fanatic to get results. If you work progressively harder over time and look at the big picture, then you can get results and still keep your sanity. Often, people go 100 percent all-in and create a miserable lifestyle that is set up for failure. You are miserable because you have to exercise all the time, go on a 100 percent strict diet, and never eat the foods that you like. You are unhappy and you are working at a higher level than you should be. Soon you fail. Everyone has been on that rollercoaster with their exercise or diet at sometime in their life. You had this great plan to start a balls-to-the-wall exercise program or diet, and one week into it, you quit because you were miserable. You *have* to be happy. You don't have to go all-in.

**All that you have to do is work harder than
you are already working.**

You have to improve *your* situation. Diet and exercise is relative to what *you* already do, not what is labeled as a "great workout" or a "great diet." This progressive approach will be explained in great detail in the next chapter. Don't set yourself up to fail. Just work harder than you already are and go from there. You want to get the best results possible without sacrificing the quality of your life.

Don't worry so much about losing weight.

You have to change your thinking. Is your goal to lose weight or is it to look better, feel better, and be healthier? People get so caught up in the weight loss, and it sets them up for failure. Everyone has this number in their head of a weight that they want to be. They think that they will not look good unless they weigh a certain amount. The focus is on the weight, not the results. Do you want to change your weight or would you rather just get results? I very rarely weigh my clients or myself. My goal is not to change weight. It is to change bodies. I determine results by results, not weight. The mirror tells me all that I need to know when it comes to body improvement. The way I feel tells me all I need to know when it comes to my health. The scale only tells me a number. If I can be happy with the way that I look and feel, then I don't care if I weigh 400 lbs or 175 lbs. My goal is to look good and feel good, not to weigh a certain weight. People use the weight as a judgment tool. That is the perfect set-up for failure. If you make improvements to your exercise and diet, your body and health will improve, regardless of what your weight does. If you are extremely overweight, you will lose weight, but if you are average size and just looking to get in better shape, then you may not lose weight. Muscle weighs more than fat. You may lose some fat and gain some muscle, and completely transform your body without losing any weight. I have actually had clients lose sizes in their waste and gain weight on the scale! The mental approach to weight has to change. Often, people will look in the mirror and say to themselves, "yes, I am getting results, I look better." Then they step on the scale and look at the weight and say, "oh wait, actually I am not getting results, I haven't lost any weight." After just being happy about improvements, the individual is now down and frustrated, and eventually will quit. Why? Because of a number. I am not saying that you should never weigh yourself. What I am saying is to let the mirror, the way your clothes fit, and the way you feel determine if you are getting results—not the scale.

Choose to *not* exercise and diet instead of choosing *to* exercise and diet.

The thinking is backwards for many people. The average person does not exercise or diet. Exercise is not part of his daily routine and he eats whatever he wants, whenever he wants, with no rules. Every now-and-then, this person decides to exercise, or decides to go on a diet. Basically, he will choose *to* exercise that day or week or choose *to* eat better that day or week. It is not a regular part of his life. He chose to do it, the same as he chooses to read a book or to watch a television series. You have to make exercise and diet a regular part of your life so it becomes automatic—becomes daily. If you exercise and diet regularly, then occasionally you can choose *not* to exercise, choose to take a break. If you normally eat good, then occasionally, on a weekend or at a party or just at a random time, you can choose *not* to eat good. Make going to the gym a part of your day. Don't work 8:00 to 5:00 then go home. Your day should be 8:00 to 6:00 with the last hour at the gym or you can go to the gym on your way to work each day, or on your lunch break, whatever works for you; just make it a part of your day. (Lunch breaks are a great time, because not only are you exercising, you are avoiding going out to lunch!) Make exercising automatic. Make it a habit. Then it will be no big deal if you decide to take an occasional day off or a week off once or twice a year. If you go to the gym everyday after work and one day you decide to meet a friend for dinner after work instead of going to the gym, then it is no big deal for you to miss that one visit to the gym.

Unfortunately, most people are the opposite. They always do something other than exercise after work, and every once in a while, they will decide *to* go to the gym. The thinking has to be reversed. I eat good and exercise on a daily basis, but occasionally I will choose not to exercise one day or I will choose not to eat healthy one day for lunch or one night for dinner. You have to make exercise a part of your daily routine. It's ok to miss a day of exercise or to eat a cheat meal. You have to look at the big picture. If you look at each week, month, and year as a whole, overall you should do well. And, if at the end of the week, month, or year you can look back and feel good about the overall, then you should be getting results.

You have to find your motivation.

Motivation and determination supersedes everything. Tired? Hungry? If you are motivated enough, then you can get past things that will cause you to fail. You can operate on less sleep if you are motivated enough. You can get through hunger if you are motivated enough. I am not saying that you can never be tired or sleepy after a night of little sleep, or hungry if you miss a meal. What I am saying is not to let those things be barriers. I workout every morning, regardless of whether I am tired or not. If I am tired, it doesn't mean that I will not exercise. It just means that it may be a little more difficult that day. My motivation is to be in the best shape in the world. That trumps everything else. I am determined because of that motivating factor. Sleep and hunger may be valid excuses, but they aren't as great as my motivation. You have to find your motivation. Is it to look good? Is it to feel better? Is it a warning sign from a doctor? Is it to be a better parent and role model? Whatever it may be, you have to find it. Don't just diet and exercise because you know that you are supposed to. Do it because you want to!

Don't think the negative. You are just planting a seed for failure.

Let's say that you work late and you don't have time to exercise after work. You are used to sleeping-in in the mornings before going to work, but if you want to exercise, then your only option is to exercise very early in the morning. You start getting up very early to exercise and you are very tired. You aren't used to this amount of sleep. You are tired for two reasons. You are tired because you are getting less sleep than you normally get and you are tired because you *think* you should be tired after waking up earlier than normal. Your mind is telling your body to be tired. You made the decision to be tired before you even went to bed. Knowing that you were only going to get a certain amount of sleep, you geared your thinking to tell you that you would be tired the next morning. A little self-psych trick that I do is to set my alarm well before I go to bed, and I don't really look at the clock when I finally get in bed. I don't know exactly when I fall asleep, so I don't know exactly how much sleep that I am going to get. When I wake up, I let my feelings tell me if I am tired or not, not a preconceived notion from the night before. I am not saying that you can't be tired. All I am saying is to let your feelings tell you if you are tired, not your mind. There are many situations, like the sleep example, that you either can mentally get around, or at least make easier. A lot of this diet and exercise stuff is in your head. You create mental barriers. You have the power to change your thinking. People will create excuses, like being tired, to get out of exercising, or like being hungry, to get out of having to eat good. These barriers can be beat. You have the power in your mind to beat them. I could go into literally hundreds of excuses that I have heard over the years, some valid, some ridiculous. All of which *can* be overcome. My all-time favorite is "I am gonna start coming to the gym; I'm just waiting until I get in a little better shape before I do." I also like the excuse, "Oh I eat good, I eat lots of fruits and vegetables; I don't need to improve my diet." In the exercise portion of this book, I discuss more excuses and ways around them.

CHAPTER THREE

Step by Step – A Progressive Approach

Exercise, diet, health, and wellness are actually not *that* difficult. People fail because they start at too high a level. People make two very critical mistakes. First, they work too hard too fast. Second, they view their diet and exercise results in the short-term. People try too hard to get their results in too short of a time period—the "lose 30 lbs in thirty days idea." Health and wellness is not a short-term project. You can't work hard, get your results, and then quit. Exercising and eating well have to be done forever. This is a **lifestyle**. Take a look at the ten most fit people that you know. They didn't get the results that they wanted and then quit and keep their results. They exercise and eat well on a daily basis.

Just about everyone in the world has been on the same rollercoaster of diet and exercise. You start an exercise program and you kill yourself to get results until you quickly realize that you can't keep up the pace, you are miserable, and you were happier before you exercised. So, a month into it, you quit. The same situation happens with your diet. You become extremely motivated with an all-or-nothing diet and two weeks into it you are starving and not eating foods that you like, so you quit and go back to eating junk food and not dieting at all. You continue to eat badly and not exercise for a couple of months until you start feeling bad or guilty again, then you go *all-in* again for a few weeks, once again, too hard on the exercise and too strict on the diet. Then you quit again. This rollercoaster will never end until you make the appropriate "lifestyle" changes.

It's all relative to you.

You have to take a different approach. Your new commitment is great, but you need to be committed to improving gradually, and making exercise and healthier eating a part of your life. All that you have to do is improve *your* situation. Your situation is *your* exercise and diet. Don't go on a diet. Don't go on a specific, over-the-top, exercise program. Improve your own diet. Improve your own exercise routine. All you have to do is do better than you were doing previously. Exercise more than you were exercising and eat better than you were eating. You will get results this way, and over time, if you keep improving *your* situation, you will keep getting results. This will work as long as you are always improving.

Do *good* forever, not *great* for a little while.

Your goal should be to do good forever, not great for a short period of time and then bad for a longer period, then great for a short period again, then bad again, and so on. Live by a percentage rule, such as eighty-twenty. Eat good and exercise 80 percent of the time, and eat bad and be lazy 20 percent of the time. Do 80 percent forever, not 100 percent for a short period of time. Eighty percent for twelve months is better than alternating 100 percent for two months with 0 percent for two months, which results 50 percent good and 50 percent bad for the entire year. Do "good" the majority of the time, not all the time. That is the *ultimate* goal.

The good news is that you don't necessarily have to start off doing "good" the majority of the time. You only have to do good *more* than you already are doing. If you normally only exercise and eat good 10 percent of the time, then you don't have to start at 80 percent. Start by exercising and eating good 20 percent of the time. (Remember, it is a progressive plan). This way is extremely easy and you *will* see results, because you just improved your situation by 10 percent. When the results stop, improve more. Up your level to 30 percent good and 70 percent bad. Repeat this process until you get to an eighty-twenty split.

Take baby steps.

Improved health and fitness needs to be done gradually. The results will be better and will last longer. We all want quick fixes and instant gratification, but in the fitness world, it is a lifetime body of work. Treat your exercise and diet programs like they are levels or "stairs." If you make changes and improvements in small increments, then you will never notice the difference between each increment. This way requires little discipline, thus providing little misery. My favorite analogy is that of a staircase. There are stairs going from the ground floor to the second floor, which is about twelve feet above. If you try to jump to the second floor, it is literally impossible. If you try to stack four-foot-tall blocks up, then you can make it up by climbing up three giant steps, but it will be very difficult, and you will probably give up during the climbing process. If you take small, six-inch increment stairs, you can make it to the second floor very easily. Six inches is a very easy step. You make it to the second level without noticing that you just elevated twelve feet. Your mind and body do not mind a six-inch improvement. It requires little effort. You don't burn out. The first two steps were the same degree of difficulty as the last two steps. Take this approach with your diet and exercise.

You can also think of this as levels. Go from level one to level two, then from two to three and then three to four, and so on. Don't try to start at level one hundred! Start at level one and you will see results…and it will be easy. When your results slow and you get used to level one, then proceed to level two. Eventually, you will go from level ninety-nine to one hundred, which is the same increment as going from level one to two! How does all this apply to exercise? The following example can help explain: You will get results if you run twenty minutes straight. Well, you don't normally do that and you can barely run at all. Start by running one minute and walking nineteen minutes. That is one minute more running than you are used to, so you will get something out of it. The next day or week, run two minutes and walk eighteen, which is not too much more difficult. Then increase to three minutes running and seventeen minutes walking, then four and sixteen, and so on, until you are able to run twenty minutes. Don't try to go from running zero minutes to running twenty minutes the first day.

A diet example is this: You normally drink four soft drinks per day. You know that if you stop, you will lose body fat. Don't try to go from four to zero. Improve from four to three. You just cut out close to 200 calories and 40 grams (g) of sugar per day. You can loose a pound of body fat in about fifteen days just by making that one change, *and you still get to drink three soft drinks per day!* When you get used to three per day, then cut back to two, and so on, until you have eliminated non-diet soft drinks from your diet. By the time that you are at zero soft drinks per day, you will have gone from one to zero, instead of four to zero. It is much easier this way.

Specific diet and exercise will be discussed in much more details in the following chapters. The point is to increase over a long period of time gradually instead of drastically increasing over a short period of time and burning out. **Take baby steps.**

You don't have to exercise all the time and eat good all the time. Just do them the majority of the time. Look at the day as a whole, the week as a whole, and the year as a whole. As long as you do good the majority of the time, and you are gradually improving, then you will always be obtaining results. Looking better, feeling better, and being healthy is a lifelong project.

IV.
DIET – *LOOK GOOD AND STILL EAT PIZZA!*

CHAPTER ONE

Introduction

Eat this; eat that. Don't eat this; don't eat that. Try this diet; try that one. Etcetera, etcetera, etcetera. Dieting can be confusing. It can be bad. It can be miserable. There is good news though—it doesn't have to be those things. This book is all about gradual and easy. This book is about keeping it simple. This book will teach you how to improve your diet to get results and still be happy. This approach is about avoiding misery!

There is one very important rule that virtually everyone who tries a diet breaks. That rule is "If you don't like it, then don't eat it." Too often, people go on diets and they are miserable. They try to eat stuff that they don't like and they never get to eat stuff that they do like. If you apply the principles learned in this book, then you will always be improving your diet, *and* you will still be able to enjoy the foods that you like on a regular basis. Avoid misery. Change your thinking. The way that you have been trying to diet for years has not worked. It's time to try a different, but practical, approach to dieting.

CHAPTER TWO

History and Trends

Human diet has changed and changed and changed again since the beginning of time. Like everything in life, we can look back on history and use it to improve the future. There are really only two major diet trends that I want to get into in this book, the **fat-free** craze of the early to mid 90s and the **low-carb** craze of the late 90s and early 2000s.

During the fat free era, people ate tons of anything and everything, as long as it was labeled "fat free." Thousands of extra calories were consumed because of this, as were thousands of extra grams of sugar. Remember, fat free is "fat" free, not sugar free, or calorie free. I remember eating entire fat-free cakes when I was in college in the mid 1990s. There was one particular chocolate cake that was fat free that I loved. To this day, it is one of the best cakes I have ever had. Looking back, it tasted *so* good for a reason. It had hundreds of grams of sugar in it and well over 1000 calories. It may not have had any fat in it, but it definitely was *fattening*. I would eat a fairly healthy dinner and then pig out on this cake just about every night. I gave myself the green light to eat as much as I wanted because I thought that since it was "fat-free," it was ok to eat. Remember, some fat-free foods, usually desserts, may be fat free, but are still fattening because they are loaded with sugar and calories. Excess sugar and calorie intake can lead to excess body fat. These foods are fat free by definition only. They can actually be the very opposite of fat free. A 12-ounce (oz) soft drink is fat free, but it is one of the most fattening items that you can consume. An average 12-oz can of soft drink has about 150 calories and close to 40 g of sugar. That is only a 12-oz can. Most people get a 20-oz bottle when they get a soft drink!

Later in this book, I will talk about fat-free and low-fat foods that can be beneficial. They do have good value when you are talking about regular foods like salad dressings, butter, milk, cheese, and so on, because these types of fat-free or low-fat foods are lower in calories. When you are talking about sweets and foods that contain a lot of sugar, then usually fat free doesn't help you much, because the lack of fat is usually covered up by a lot of sugar. Most of the problems and misconceptions of food comes from marketing and advertising. Companies want to fool people into buying their product. They are concerned with selling products, not with people eating well. Popsicles and gummy candies are a good example. They often have "fat free" written on the package to entice the consumer. People will purchase these items because they think they are OK to eat and they will eat as much as they want. The reality is that popsicles and gummy candies are fat free. They always have been. But...they are fattening. They are loaded with sugar. Be careful and watch out for clever marketing and advertising. Remember, just because it says "fat free" doesn't mean that it is not fattening.

So everyone got fat eating fat-free foods and we realized that this wasn't working. That led us into our next food fad, the low-carbohydrate trend of the late 90s and early 2000s. During this fad, people ate low or no carbohydrates, but loaded up on fat. All the bacon and grease you wanted!

Sounds great doesn't it? Just like the fat-free cake seemed OK. There is a catch though. Eliminating carbohydrates and eating high fat foods led to high body fat, high cholesterol, heart disease, vitamin deficiencies, and various other health problems. Depleting your carbohydrate intake means not eating potatoes, cereals, breads, fruits and vegetables, and many other nutrient-containing foods. Another problem is that your body *prefers* to burn carbohydrates for energy, and if you don't have any carbohydrates to burn for energy, then you may feel weak and tired.

With these diet trends, it is all about the marketing. Foods can be labeled fat free or "low carb" and they will fly off the shelves. Just because something is labeled "low carb" doesn't mean that it is good for you. Bacon is low in carbohydrates, but is loaded with fat and calories. Don't fall victim to marketing schemes. Educate yourself on fat and carbohydrates so that you will know when to eat reduced-fat or fat-free products and when to eat low-carb products.

It is important to reduce fat and carbohydrates to reduce calories, but you never want to eliminate any one nutrient group. Your body needs balance. A good balance is needed to create a healthy eating lifestyle. As stated before and again in this book in detail, "it's all about the calories!"

CHAPTER THREE

Avoid Misery – Take a Progressive Approach

Are you sick of going on a diet? Are you miserable? Have you been yo-yo dieting? Are you on the never-ending rollercoaster of going on and off diets? Most people will answer yes to any or all of those questions. Let's start with the term **diet**. The term diet literally means anything that you eat. If you eat pizza and hot dogs, then you are on a pizza and hot dogs diet. Many people don't use the term the correct way. Diet is not the best term to use, especially when you talk about "going on a diet." "Going on a diet" suggests a beginning. If there is a beginning, then chances are there is an end. Well, unfortunately, with dieting there is no end. You can't start a diet and continue for one month or until you get results and then quit. Actually, you can, but your results will go away. So, instead of "going on" a diet, let's look at "improving" your diet. Let's develop a "healthy eating lifestyle." The bad news is that this is a lifelong thing. The good news is that it never has to be 100 percent strict. The roller coaster of dieting (great for one month, quit for two months, great again, etc.) is not the answer. It is too strict. It is miserable. You never get to eat the foods that you like. Instead of trying to eat great for a month and then bad for two months and on and on, try to eat good for an entire year. Instead of *great* for a short period of time, do *good* for a long period of time. Your result is better this way. You can't fad diet forever. Usually fad diets have to end for one of two different reasons. Most fad diets deplete a certain nutrient category, like carbs or fat. Because you are deprived of certain nutrients, you will eventually see health ramifications from the depletion. The other reason the fad diet will end is that you will get sick of it. There is some food that you like to eat that is not allowed on that particular fad diet and you want it so badly that you quit. All that being said, if you want to continue seeing results, then you eventually have to learn to eat right. Eating right is not eating perfect. It is not being miserable. Eating right is eating good, and still being happy. You have to have some discipline, but not 100 percent discipline.

Don't eat good? That's great news!

It is all relative to what you currently are doing. The "good" that we have been talking about is the end result. The beginning of developing a "healthy eating lifestyle" is just improving on what you are currently doing. Start by making one change. Your body will notice one change; your mind will not if it is a small enough change. Then a week later, make another change. Keep making small changes week after week. Take the stairs! Take baby steps. Do this gradually and it will be easy. You will not see results as quick, but you will be less likely to quit and you will see more results in the long run. Let's revisit the scenario given earlier in the book for an example:

John eats horrible and drinks four 12-oz cans of soda per day. Instead of quitting soda all together, he reduces from four cans of soda to three per day, a small change that required little discipline. That is the only change that he made in his entire diet. He still eats badly everyday and drinks three cans of soda. He has cut out roughly 750 calories and 250 g of sugar per week. That is enough to lose a pound of body fat in three to four weeks. That is just making that one change. You obviously could make a few more changes and start exercising to see results even faster, but don't change too much. You want to keep it easy. You want to be happy.

The good thing about progression is that it is always easy and you are always improving.

Let's look at all this in percentages. The ultimate goal is to eat good maybe 80 to 90 percent of the time, never 100 percent. All you have to do is improve what *you* do. If you eat good 0 percent of the time, then all you have to do is eat good 10 percent of the time and you will get results. Then, when the results slow, you improve to eating good 20 percent of the time, and improve again when the results slow. On and on you keep improving over time until you are at 80 or 90 percent good—never 100 percent good. You need the bad 10 to 20 percent; it will keep you going. The progression is to go from 70 to 80 percent, not from zero to 80 percent. Remember, you don't need to improve too much too fast because you will burn out AND YOU WILL BE MISERABLE!

Be honest with yourself about your diet. It is a good thing if your diet is poor in the beginning. That means that there is a lot of room for improvement and a lot of changes that can be made. You can pick and choose what you change at this level. It is much more difficult to improve a perfect diet than it is to improve a bad one. Make gradual changes.

People will often think that having a good diet means 100 percent strict, but actually, a good diet is a good balance of good and bad. It is good the *majority* of the time, not *all* the time. You are just about as likely to see me eating pizza as you will see me eating grilled chicken! If you do good the majority of the time, you will see results. You have to be happy. Don't go so strict that you are miserable. If you are not happy, then it is not worth it.

CHAPTER FOUR

It's All about the Calories

It's all about the calories. That sounds complicated. That sounds difficult. It is supposed to be easy. You mean, "I have to count every calorie that I eat and burn?" Not exactly. Being "all about the calories" actually is the easiest way to diet and it can be that way without having to count calories. We need to focus on calories, but we don't necessarily have to count calories. We have to lower them. Your goal each day is to burn more calories than you eat. You have two sides to improve, the burning-calories side, which is exercise, and the consuming-less-calories side, which is diet. Whatever your diet and exercise is right now represents and even line on both sides, like in the diagram below:

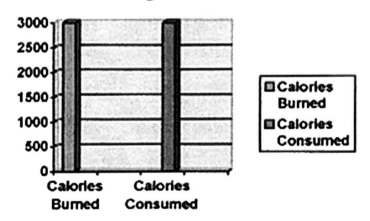

*The calorie totals are just a number to use.
Yours may be different, but the ratio is the same.

At the end of the day, you want to burn more than you eat. You want to burn more *through* exercise and eat less by cutting calories. By burning more and eating less, your chart would look like the diagram below:

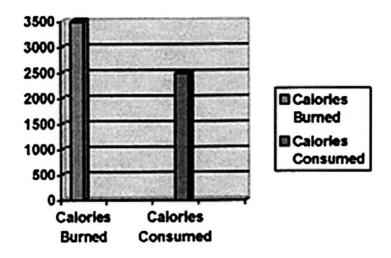

The above illustration represents a 1000-calorie deficit, which means that you *burned* 1ooo more calories than you *ate*. It doesn't matter if the above chart is 2500 to 1500 or 4500 to 3500; all that really matters is the 1000-calorie deficit. Your totals are irrelevant. The deficit is what is important. It really is simple; if you burn more than you eat, you will lose body fat. So, how can you cut calories without counting them? There is a little bit of counting that needs to take place, but you don't have to count every calorie that you burn or every calorie that you eat. Later in the book, we will talk about ways to burn calories through exercise, but for now, just remember; if you exercise more than you normally do, you will burn more than you normally do, thus increasing the *burn* side. For the diet side, if you eat less than you normally do, you will decrease the amount of calories that you consume, thus decreasing the *consume* side.

It is all relative to what you *normally* do, so it doesn't matter what the totals are. All that matters is an improvement on each side of the calorie chart. The only calorie counting you need to do involves looking at certain foods that you normally eat and finding ways to cut calories. There are two easy ways to cut calories: (1) eat the same food, but eat less of it and (2) to eat the same amount of food, but choose foods lower in calories. If you normally eat a cheeseburger for lunch, you can reduce your calories either way. You can eat half of the cheeseburger, which will give you half of the calories, and you still get to eat a cheeseburger. Or, you can eat a grilled chicken sandwich instead of the cheeseburger, which will give you a calorie reduction and you still get to eat the same amount of food. The cheeseburger example allows you to eat the *same* food, and the grilled chicken example allowed you to eat the same *amount* of food. In the beginning stages of your progression, either way is beneficial, so choose which ever way gets your calories down the easiest. Eventually, you may want to take the healthier option (grilled chicken over cheeseburger), but at first it does not matter very much. Pick and choose ways to reduce your calories throughout the day. Do it gradually. Base everything off what *you normally do.* Start with one change, like switching to diet drinks from regular, and there is your first calorie reduction. Get used to that one change and then make another, and so on.

The counting of calories is not wearing a pedometer and counting every calorie that you burn and it is not counting every calorie that you eat. The counting of calories is counting individual meals or foods, so that you know that you are making a reduction. It doesn't matter as much if you ate 3000 calories in one day. What matters is if you lowered your intake by 200 calories. Basically, if you cut out a soft drink from your diet, you will cut 2oo calories out of it. It doesn't matter if you went from 3000 to 2800 or from 4000 to 3800. What matters is the 200-calorie reduction.

You *can* eat at night and you *don't* have to eat six times a day!

There are several diet concepts that you don't necessarily have to follow. One of these concepts is that it is bad for you (or fattening) to eat at night. This is not necessarily true. The root of that thought process is that by eating late at night, your food will not be burned, resulting in it being stored in your body as fat. If you or someone you know lost weight from not eating late at night, they probably lost weight because of the "not eating" part of it, not because of *when* they didn't eat. Basically, by cutting out a meal, that person cut out a significant portion of their calories and as a result, lost weight and body fat. It didn't really have anything to do with not eating at night. It was just from *not eating*. You look at the daily totals and if you can lower them, it doesn't really matter when you eat them. Consider the following two examples. They are different paths to the same result:

> **Example 1:** If you go from eating four meals per day to three meals by cutting out your last meal and reducing your daily total by 350 calories, you will lose 1 lb of body fat in ten days.
> **Example 2:** If you go from eating four meals per day to three by cutting out breakfast and you reduce your daily total by 350 calories, you will lose 1 lb of body fat in ten days.

Both examples yielded the same results. The point is, if it makes you happier to reduce your calories earlier in the day instead of at night, do so. None of this will work if you are miserable, so make the changes that make you the most happy.

Another thing that people are confused about is the rule of having to eat six meals per day. Yes, ideally, it would be good to eat maybe four to six times per day split up equally. This would help maintain energy levels and keep your metabolism running, but it can also hinder your progress. Many times, people will be eating two or three times per day and then hear from some so-called "fitness expert" on the news say that they should eat six times per day. So what do those people do? They go from eating three times per day to six times, *by adding three meals*. They add three meals; thus, they add 1000 calories to their daily total, all because they think they have to eat six times per day. In that example, they gained weight by eating six times per day. People use this as an excuse to eat more. The bottom line is the calories, so if you eat fewer calories during a day by eating fewer meals, then eat fewer meals! The benefits of the fewer calories far outweigh the benefits of eating more times per day.

Another problem that people have is eating breakfast. Don't get me wrong here. Breakfast *is* important, and it can do a lot for you. Once again, people use the thought of "you have to eat breakfast" as a crutch, as a green light to eat a huge calorie-filled breakfast. Breakfast is important. It can balance your blood sugar in the morning. It can get your metabolism running well for the day, and it can make you feel energized. What breakfast does is "break" the "fast" that your body is in from the previous night of sleep. The problem is that people are consuming too many calories. If you eat a bowl of bran cereal or plain oatmeal or hard-boiled eggs is one thing, but if you eat a sausage biscuit because "you are supposed to eat breakfast" then you've got it all wrong. Skipping breakfast can benefit people that are very overweight and in high-risk categories for heart disease, stroke, diabetes, and so on, due to their weight. The benefits of the calorie reduction of missing breakfast, which are losing weight and reducing serious health risks, far outweigh the benefits that you get from a good healthy breakfast. I am not saying never to eat breakfast. What I am saying is not to use breakfast as an excuse to eat more. Remember, it's all about the calories.

I consider myself to be in great shape. I stay around 5 percent body fat and maintain good strength, athletic ability, and endurance. I also don not have any major health problems. My blood pressure, cholesterol, and other indicators all check very well. That being said, the following statements may surprise you:

> *I rarely eat breakfast.*
> *I rarely eat more than twice per day.*
> *I eat most of my calories at night.*

I am not saying that you have to (or need to) do these things. I am just showing you that you can do these things and still be in very good shape and healthy. I am showing you that you don't have to do all the hard-core fitness expert rules to get results.

I do cardio every morning on an empty stomach. I drink some coffee, which is calorie free, and I get my energy from the caffeine to do my cardio. When I do my cardio, I am burning stored calories. I used to eat a bowl of oatmeal for breakfast, and then do cardio. By doing it that way, I had to burn the 250 calories form the oatmeal before I even got my "stored" calories. So even if I ate a lot the night before, I am usually burning a lot of it the next morning. Another thing that I do not do is eat several times per day. As a part of my progression of calorie reduction over the years, I started to reduce each meal. Over time, I started eating fewer meals. I would rather eat 2000 calories in one day by having the bulk of them at night than eat 3000 calories per day split up evenly. The evenly split day is more difficult for me *and* it produces more calories! Why would I want to eat more times per day if I am not as happy and get less result? I would rather really enjoy one meal and not worry about the others than to eat six meals in a day and not enjoy any of them! Another problem that I have with eating a lot during the day is that it actually makes me feel more tired and have less energy. It causes my blood sugar to rise and fall. Remember, it's all relative to your situation and your improvements. I went from eating three bad meals per day to five good meals and got results. But eventually I evolved into eating fewer meals throughout the day. **I am in better shape now than I was when I ate four to six times per day.** It is all relative to what *you* normally do, and it is important to make changes in a way that keeps you as happy as possible. Also, don't forget, it's all about the calories.

CHAPTER FIVE

Don't Forget to Cheat –
It's Good for You!

When speaking about diet, I refer to eating a bad meal as a "cheat meal." You may also have heard the term "cheat day" referring to an entire day of cheating. I like to keep it in terms of meals and not days. A cheat meal can be anything you want—a bad meal, no rules. It is very important to cheat. If you don't cheat, you will never be happy. I eat good *so* I can eat bad. It is a rewards system. You eat good and then you reward yourself with a cheat meal. Eating good is for your body. Eating bad is for your mind and for your sanity. It's not worth it if you never get to enjoy eating.

Traditionally, I would say to follow this example: eat good and exercise throughout the week, and cheat and rest some on the weekends. The reason is that you eat good while you are exercising because your food is your fuel for your body and you want good fuel in your body for your exercise. Then, on the weekends, you let your body rest from exercise and your mind rest from dieting. That is a good plan to follow, but it is not the *only* way to do it.

You can cheat some during the week and less on the weekends if you want to. I have a certain number of cheat meals per week that I usually allow myself. I like to space them out a little, but I definitely have more of them on the weekends. I always have a cheat meal on Sunday night. Why? Well, it is a reward for a good week, and, more importantly, it makes me wake up Monday morning feeling motivated to get back to eating healthy and exercising. I don't do many cheat days where I cheat for an entire day. Traditional cheat days allow for **three** cheat meals in one day! I would rather have three days with one cheat meal each day. I would enjoy those days more and each cheat meal more that way.

Another good thing about cheating is that cheat foods taste much better when you don't have them all of the time. Trust me, if you eat junk food all of the time, you take it for granted how good it tastes. If you eat dessert every night, you don't enjoy it as much as if you eat it only two times per week.

The great thing about the cheat meal system is that you never have to go without eating something that you enjoy. If you go on a diet that never allows French fries and you love French fries, then you will never make it through that diet. I can have French fries once or twice a week if I want. I just don't have them *every day*. There still is some discipline. You have to have enough discipline not to eat bad every day, but not so much that you have to avoid a certain craving forever.

If you're gonna cheat, then cheat!

People often waiver along a line of never really eating good and never really cheating, they try to eat healthy but still have a touch of something bad or that *one* cookie after dinner. Or, they will try to cheat, but feel bad, so they don't really eat what they wanted. Neither way will make you happy or get results. It is a rewards system. If you eat good and earn your cheats, then cheat. *If you're gonna cheat, then cheat!* Don't eat that *one* cookie every night and never really enjoy it, then feel guilty for eating it. Wait until your cheat meal and eat several cookies. When you do the one cookie per night example, you never really enjoy it because you always want more. Not only are you not happy eating the one cookie, you wasted those calories! It is a lose-lose situation. When you have done good and earned a cheat, then you can eat more than one cookie and be very satisfied. Your calories will not matter because you earned it, and you will be happier, thus producing a win-win situation.

More Good = More Bad

The better you eat, the worse you get to eat. Think of it as a reward system. The better you do, the bigger the reward. Another thing that I do is try to eat a certain amount of cheat meals each week and do a certain amount of cardio each week. On weeks where I may cheat more than normal, I do more cardio than normal. It can help cancel out the extra cheat. That also allows me to break from my normal rules a little if needed. Remember, it's all relative to you and what you normally do. If you normally have three cheat meals per week and do cardio four times per week and you have a situation where you cheated an extra time, then just do an extra cardio that week. That week would end up being four cheat meals and five cardio workouts. Give yourself the option to make adjustments when needed. The enjoyment of the extra cheat meal far outweighs the work of the extra cardio.

Have you ever been in a situation where you were at a restaurant trying to eat healthy because it is not one of your scheduled cheat meals? You are turning down the bread, ordering some meal that you don't want, and skipping dessert, all because it is not your normal time to cheat. You are miserable. I am sure that has happened to many people who are trying to eat a good diet. I try never to go to a restaurant where I have to avoid eating what I want. So, if I normally eat good on Tuesdays and I get a call to go to a birthday dinner on a Tuesday night, then that night I will go to the party and I will cheat. I then have two choices. I can cheat one less time later in the week when I normally would cheat or I can do extra cardio to make up for it. Remember, it's all about calories burned versus calories consumed, so you have two sides with which to work.

The ultimate goal is to eat good the majority of the time and cheat the minority of the time—maybe 80 percent good and 20 percent bad. You eventually want to get to this eighty-twenty split, or better. Right now, you only need to be better than *you* normally are. If you have no rules on eating, eat whatever you want whenever you want, eat three meals per day, and you are cheating all three meals, you are cheating twenty-one times per week. If you reduce to two cheat meals per day and one non-cheat, you will be cheating fourteen times per week. You will see results and you still get to eat fourteen cheat meals per week. Now eventually those results will slow down, and to get more results you will have to improve again and go from two cheat meals per day to one cheat meal and two healthy meals, You would see more results and you are still getting to cheat one time per day! . When those results slow or stop, then you would improve by cheating every other day, and so on, until you reached your eighty-twenty split or better. If you eat twenty meals per week and you try to eat good 80 percent of the time, you still get four cheat meals. You get to indulge four times per week! There is not as much discipline to dieting as you may have thought. At the end of the week, you want to be at a certain mark, like the eighty-twenty. You have all week to figure it out, so don't worry if you mess up on a Monday. Instead of saying to yourself, "Oh well, the damage is done, I will eat bad all week," just make up for it, and at the end of the week, be where you need to be. Look at the big picture. Look at the day as a whole, the week as a whole, and even the month and the year as a whole.

CHAPTER SIX

You Don't Have to Suffer Through the Good Part of Your Diet

We have established that you want to try to eat good the majority of the time and cheat the minority of the time. If there are no rules on cheating, then cheating is simple—eat whatever you want (within some reason, of course!). What about knowing what to eat during the *majority* of your diet? You don't have to suffer through the good part of your diet. I will show you how to make better choices and enjoy it as much as possible.

Let's start with nutrition basics, somewhat of a crash-course in nutrition. I do want to keep it simple though. I am not trying to give you a degree in nutrition or certify you as a dietician. What I am going to do is tell you some basic nutrition information so that you will have a better understanding of what foods you are eating, why you are eating them, and how much of them you should be eating.

The key nutrients that we are going to look at, very generally, are protein, carbohydrates, fat, and water. Protein is the building blocks for your muscle. Protein also helps with development of bones, teeth, hair, skin, and nails. The most protein is found in meats, dairy, and eggs. Protein is also found in many other foods, but not in large amounts. How much protein is found in these foods? We will use averages to keep things simple. Four ounces of meat, being chicken, beef, pork, and we will even include fish in this, on average, contain about 20 to 25 g of protein. An 8-oz glass of milk on average contains about 8 g of protein. One large egg usually has about 7 g of protein. Usually you can read on the nutrition label to find out how much protein is in a certain food, but for times that you don't have access to a label, you can use these averages to figure out how much protein you are eating. How much protein should you get per day? That can vary based on your weight and muscle-building goals. A good rule of thumb is to try to get 50 to 75 percent of your bodyweight in grams per day. Example: if you weigh 150 lbs, then try to get 75 to 110 g. If you wanted to build more muscle, then you can eat more than that, but remember, the more protein that you eat, the more calories you are consuming, and as stated before, *it's all about the calories.* You can still build muscle and get stronger without having to consume hundreds and hundreds of grams of protein.

Carbohydrates supply the body with energy. They are the body's preferred fuel source. Your body wants to use carbs to burn fuel for energy. Over the past several years, carbohydrates have been looked at as bad and the reason for weight gain. People thought that they were getting fat because of eating carbohydrates. People went on all kinds of "no-carb" diets to lose weight. Some people did lose weight, but it wasn't necessarily because of the carb cutting. It was because of the calorie deficit that was reached by cutting out the foods that contained carbohydrates. There is a problem though. When you eliminate carbohydrates from your diet, you eliminate many valuable nutrients from your diet. These no-carb diets lack the nutrients found in fruits and vegetables, potatoes, breads, rice, cereals, to name a few. One of the things stressed in this book is BALANCE. You want a balance; so eliminating carbohydrates throws off your balance. You want to cut the bad carbs and continue to eat the good carbs, day or night—it doesn't matter when. What matters is the calorie total at the end of the day. Try to stick to good carbohydrates like whole wheat and whole grain breads and pastas, brown rice, sweet potatoes, oatmeal, and fruits and vegetables. Try to limit the bad carbohydrates, like white breads and sugars, to your cheat meals.

The fat category can be a little confusing. The fat in foods has some good qualities and some bad. Fat carries vitamins into the body and helps with feelings of fullness. But, unfortunately, fat is very high in calories and cholesterol. One gram of fat contains 9 calories. To compare, 1 g of protein only has 4 calories and 1 gram of carbohydrate only has 4 calories. The main reason that I suggest eating a lot of fat-free and low-fat foods is because these foods are lower in calories—remember, *it's all about the calories*. Don't get too confused with, or worried about, which fats and how much of each fat to eat—good fats or bad fats. Keep it simple. Try to choose foods low in trans-fats and low in saturated fats. Foods with little or no amounts of trans-fats are usually easy to find because they usually are labeled as "no trans-fat" to be appealing to the customer. You can determine the amounts of the saturated fats in foods by looking at the nutrition label. If you want to try to get your "good" fats, then try to eat fish, extra virgin olive oil, or look into fish oil supplements and/or omega supplements.

The last nutrient that I want to talk about is water. Water is probably the most important aspect of your diet. Water is the only perfect product that you can consume. Water has no downside and only positive qualities. There are many benefits to drinking water. Below are some of the most important ones:

Water is calorie free. *Have as much as you like!* (Don't like it? Get in the habit of drinking it and your taste buds will change. You will grow to like it)

Water is absolutely essential for life. Where there is no water, there is no life. It's that simple.

Water transports substances in the body.

Water keeps our body temperature within normal range.

Water carries out waste through the kidneys.

Water rids your body of impurities and toxins.

Water can speed up your metabolism.

Water can increase your energy.

Water is *crucial* for hydration.

If you drink a lot of **water**, you will feel better. You will be ridding your body of stuff it doesn't want and filling it with what it really needs.

The recommended daily amount of water is 64 ozs. That should be your first goal. If you do not get at least 64 ozs per day, start with that. After you are used to drinking 64 ozs per day, then try to drink even more per day, especially if you are active. You really need more than the average 64 ozs per day if you exercise. Try to get 100 ozs or more. I usually drink at least one gallon per day. When you are trying to increase your daily water intake, do it gradually. If you normally drink 30 ozs per day, try to drink 40 per day until it gets easy, then move to 50 ozs, etcetera. Another great thing about water is that it is calorie free and when you are drinking water, you are not drinking something else that is worse for you.

Now that we have the nutrition basics covered, let's talk about real food and eating. This book will not tell you exactly what to eat, but what it will do is teach you how to make better choices and give you some ideas of changes that can be made. When trying to eat healthy, remember the most important rule: *if you don't like it, then don't eat it.* Too many times, I have seen people who thought that they had to eat plain grilled chicken and plain broccoli to be fit and improve their health, but they couldn't stand plain grilled chicken and plain broccoli. So what do they do? Instead of finding something else healthy that they liked, they just gave up and quit trying to eat healthy all together. Eating good requires some effort and some trial and error. If you don't like something, then find something else that is good for you that you like. Trust me; there is stuff out there that you will like. In situations where you just can't find something that you like, you can tough it out for a brief time period and your taste buds will change. You will end up liking that certain food.

Let's start with some easy changes to make when you are trying to make better choices:

Instead of fried foods, choose baked, grilled, or roasted. Get creative. Instead of plain grilled chicken, try marinating it in something or mixing it with some-thing. Eating well can taste good; it just requires a little effort. Save the fried foods for your cheat meals.

Instead of butter, choose fat-free spray butter. People often say to me, "the fat-free spray butter is not good for you." Well guess what? Neither is regular butter! (Often people will read a story about how a fat-free product or diet product is not good for you and they will use that as an excuse to eat the regular stuff) The fat-free spray has virtually no calories or fat. Regular butter is nothing but calories and fat. Use the fat-free spray butter to cook with or to top foods with and you will not taste the difference at all, and you will drasti-cally reduce your fat and calorie totals.

Instead of regular salad dressings, choose low-fat or fat-free salad dressing or even choose extra virgin olive oil and vinegar. The extra virgin olive oil is good for you in moderation and the vinegar is not fatten-ing. Remember this about dressings: If you like ranch dressing, then you probably will not like fat-free ranch dressing, so try a different one instead. Save the regu-lar ranch for your cheat meals. Remember, *if you don't like it, then don't eat it!*

Switch from regular cheese to 2 percent milk cheese. If you can make the switch to fat-free cheese, the by all means, do so. But, most people don't like fat free cheese, so that's why I recommend the 2 percent cheese. Two percent cheese is lower in fat and calories than regular cheese and it tastes just as good.

If you drink whole milk, switch to low-fat milk. If you drink low-fat milk, then switch to fat-free milk. Don't try to go from whole to skim. Get used to low fat, then later on reduce to skim. If you don't drink a lot of milk, but use it for cereal or to cook with, then make the switch to fat-free, you will not notice the difference, and you will reduce your fat and calories. Milk is very good for you, but it is also very fattening.

Switch from regular sour cream to light or fat-free sour cream. Most milk-based products, like sour cream, usually have good-tasting light or fat-free versions. Chances are you were eating the regular sour cream just because you *assumed* that the light would taste bad. You probably have never actually given it a fair chance.

Switch from regular bread to light bread. Ideally, switch to light wheat bread. Most regular white and wheat breads contain about 80 calories per slice; most light white and wheat breads only contain about 40 calories per slice and they taste exactly the same. Remember, just because it is "wheat" bread doesn't mean that it is low in calories. You could actually benefit by switching from regular whole wheat bread to light white bread. The 80 calorie per sandwich (40 per slice) reduction far outweighs the benefits of the importance of wheat over white. Ideally, try to choose light wheat bread; you will get the low calories *and* the health benefits.

Soft drinks—I could write an entire chapter on this one! Soft drinks are on of the most fattening things that you can put in your body. Not only are they fattening, they are also very bad for your health. In a perfect world, switch from soft drinks to water. We all know that this is no perfect world, so for the purposes of improving, switch to diet drinks. Diet drinks are not necessarily good for you, but because they are calorie-free, they are better for you than regular soft drinks. Chances are if you drink a certain regular soft drink, then you will not like the diet version. You will constantly be trying to compare the diet version to the regular version. You will be searching for that regular drink taste, and guess what—they don't taste the same! My advice is to pick a soft drink that you don't normally drink and choose the diet version of it. Then you will be basing your decision on whether or not it tastes good, not whether or not it tastes like the regular version. Plenty of diet drinks out there taste good, and some taste like the regular versions. Chances are, you will find one that you like, but if you don't, remember, you have the power to change your taste buds. It takes a while, but your tastes buds *will* change. I went until I was twenty-six years old without drinking a certain diet drink. After about one month of getting used to it, my taste buds did a complete 180-degree turn, and to this day, I like the diet better than the regular. I still recommend water, but if you must have soft drinks, choose the diet over the regular.

Switch from sweet tea to unsweet tea. Like the soft drinks, sweet tea is loaded with sugar and calories. Unsweet tea with artificial sweeteners is better for you than sugar-loaded sweet tea. Try to switch to diet green tea or plain unsweet tea instead of regular sweet tea or artificially-sweetened tea. Remember, if you train your tastes buds to drink usnweet tea, you will get used to it, and unsweet tea is actually pretty good for you.

Sports drinks are called sports drinks for a reason— they are to be used before, during, or after sports. They replenish your deep sugar energy sources that are used during activity. (They still aren't better for you than water though!) If you drink a sports drink just to drink one or because you think it is healthy, then you might as well have a regular soft drink. Sports drinks contain tons of sugar and calories and are just about as fattening as soft drinks.

What about artificial sweeteners? There is a rule in life that states that if there is a good, then there is a bad. With sugar, the good is the taste, and the bad is the fat, diabetes, and so on. With artificial sweeteners, the good is the taste and the bad is nowhere to be found? There are no calories, so that can't be the bad. They must cause cancer or some other health problems. Research after research shows no direct link between certain artificial sweeteners and cancer. Always pay attention to health studies, but remember that regular sugar is *definitely* bad for you, so it may not be a bad idea to switch to the artificial sweeteners. People usually scare themselves into avoiding artificial sweetener and end up eating too much regular sugar, then end up with health problems from the excess sugar and calories.

Try to choose baked potato chips over regular potato chips. They are the same chip, just baked instead of fried. They actually taste better in my opinion and are less greasy. Pretzels and reduced-fat wheat crackers are other good alternatives to regular potato chips.

Do you have that sweet tooth craving for dessert at night and don't want dessert during your non-cheat mealtime? Try fat-free, sugar-free pudding or gelatin. They are not fattening and actually taste very good. Remember, you get real dessert when you are cheating. This is just a recommendation to help you between cheat meals. They are not meant to be as good as regular dessert! Fat-free, sugar-free pudding has about 60 calories and sugar-free gelatin has 10 calories.

Try to switch from high-sugar cereals to high-fiber and low-sugar cereals. Don't be fooled by the name of the cereal. Read the label for the sugar content and the whole grain content. Choose cereals that are low in sugar and low in calories. Keep trying until you find one that you like. If you must sweeten it, then use some fruit or a packet of artificial sweetener, and use skim milk to mix it.

Switch from eggs to egg whites or egg white substitutes. Nearly all of the fat and calories are in the yellow part of the egg. Try to have a ratio of egg whites to egg yellows. Crack six eggs and put them into a bowl. Throw out three of the yellows and scramble the three remaining yellows with the six egg whites. You will not taste the difference and you would have just eliminated 15 g of fat and 150 calories!

Switch from regular peanut butter to reduced-fat peanut butter. Many health gurus will tell you to switch to "all-natural" peanut butter. That is fine; but remember, "all-natural" may be good for you, but reduced-fat has fewer calories, and *it's all about the calories.*

Switch from regular jelly to sugar free jelly. Jelly is loaded with sugar and is high in calories. Sugar free jellies are artificially sweetened and taste exactly the same without all the sugar and calories. You can now make an acceptable peanut butter and jelly sandwich by using light wheat bread, reduced-fat peanut butter, and sugar free jelly. I am not saying that is the most healthy sandwich in the world, but it is not bad, and compared to a regular PB&J (everything is relative in comparison to your regular diet), it is much better for you.

Switch from regular salt to low-sodium salt. Ideally, try to reduce you salt intake to a minimum, but for when you do have salt, use light salt or low-sodium salt. It tastes just as good and is much better for you. Lowering your salt intake can help fight high blood pressure and hypertension.

Switch from regular pasta to whole-wheat pasta. If you put sauce and toppings on the pasta, you will not notice the difference and the complex carbohydrates are actually good for you. You can now eat pasta and not feel guilty. For example: regular pasta sauce with lean-ground beef or chicken, onions, peppers, and whole-wheat noodles.

The above suggestions are just ideas for you to consider. The goal of my suggestions is to show you ways to reduce fat and calories without reducing taste. That creates a "no-brainer" decision. If food A and food B taste the same and food A is half the calories of food B, then it would be stupid to choose food B, thus, a "no-brainer" decision. I do not suggest just switching to the fat-free version. It may taste bad, thus requiring a lot of discipline, breaking rule one, and leading down a path that would end up causing you to give up and quit eating healthy.

The above suggestions are examples. There are literally hundreds and hundreds of choices that you can make that will make eating better easier for you. The only downside is that it will now take a little longer to shop for your groceries because you will be picking stuff up and reading all the labels!

Meal Examples

The following are some examples of meals you can eat. Each example has a bad meal, or just a regular meal, and then a "good" option for replacement. The "good" meals are good, they *are not perfect*, but they are very good *when compared* to the bad option. These are good options because they are changes you can make to *your* diet. Remember, it is all relative to what you *were* doing.

Cheeseburger and Fries

Bad: Fast-food burger and fries, or greasy, low-grade grilled burger at home with regular cheese, mayonnaise, and other condiments and deep-fried frozen French fries.

Good: 93 or 96 percent lean ground beef patties grilled at home and put on a light-wheat bun with lettuce and mustard and a little ketchup—no mayo or bacon. Add 2 percent milk cheese if you want a cheeseburger. For your French fries, cut up a raw potato into sticks and season and bake in the oven or lightly pan-fry in extra virgin olive oil. (You can also add a healthy salad to this meal.)

Spaghetti Dinner

Bad: Regular pasta, regular sauce mixed with regular ground beef, garlic loaf with cheese, and salad with ranch or Italian dressing.

Good: Whole wheat pasta, light pasta sauce mixed with 93 or 96 percent lean ground beef or chicken and chopped onions and peppers, light wheat buns toasted with fat-free butter spray and garlic salt, and salad with fat-free Italian dressing or extra virgin olive oil and vinegar.

Chicken Fingers, Rice, Fried Green Tomatoes, Squash

Bad: Heavily battered and deep fried chicken fingers and fried green tomatoes, white rice with lots of salt and butter, and cooked squash, soaked in butter.

Good: Boneless, skinless chicken tenderloins dipped in skim milk and lightly breaded with breadcrumbs and pan-fried in just a few tablespoons of extra virgin olive oil, fried green tomatoes made the same way as the chicken fingers, wild rice or brown rice, and fresh squash cooked with some fat free spray butter.

Pork Chops, Rice, Salad, and Bread

Bad: Large, fatty, grilled pork chops with white rice with regular butter and salt, salad with regular dressing, and dinner rolls covered in butter.

Good: Thin, lean, pork chops, seasoned and baked or grilled, brown rice, salad with light dressing, and light crescent rolls with fat free spray butter.

Jambalaya Meal

Bad: Jambalaya mix and regular sausage, salad with regular dressing.

Good; Jambalaya mix with light sausage or turkey sausage and boneless, skinless cooked chicken, and a salad with light or fat-free dressing.

Sloppy Joes

Bad: Sloppy joe mix and regular ground beef, regular buns, and French fries for your side.

Good: Sloppy joe mix and lean ground beef, light wheat buns and a baked potato with low-sodium salt and pepper and/or fat-free sour cream, and salad with fat-free dressing or fresh broccoli.

Taco Dinner

Bad: Taco seasoning mixed with regular ground beef and taco shells, regular cheese, regular sour cream, guacamole, etc.

Good: Taco seasoning mixed with lean ground beef or chicken and whole-wheat soft tortillas, fat-free or 2 percent cheese, fat-free sour cream, lettuce, tomatoes, and salsa.

Great: Replace the tortillas with lettuce wraps.

Pizza

Bad: Delivery pizza or regular frozen pizza

Good: Homemade pizza, whole-wheat pizza crust, pizza sauce, chunks of lean ground beef and/or chicken, shredded mozzarella cheese, onions, and peppers

Sandwich and Chips

Bad: Ham and cheese on regular white or wheat bread topped with regular cheese, mayonnaise, mustard, lettuce, tomato, oil and vinegar, and a bag of regular potato chips.

Good (option 1): Turkey and cheese on light-wheat bread topped with 2 percent cheese, mustard, lettuce, tomato, and pickles, and a bag of baked potato chips

Good (option 2): Tuna salad sandwich and a bag of baked potato chips. Make the tuna salad yourself with tuna, light or fat-free mayonnaise, and pickle relish and put on light-wheat bread. Be careful ordering tuna salad at restaurants because it is usually loaded with regular mayonnaise.

*Side trick to save even more calories when you are eating a sandwich: Make two sandwiches with the exact same ingredients, but leave the cheese off one of the sandwiches. If there are enough vegetable toppings and mustard, chances are that you will not even taste the difference in the two sandwiches. You probably will not taste the cheese because it is blanketed by the other stuff, and you will be wasting those calories. If you don't miss the cheese, then make your sandwich without it. What's the point of having those calories if you don't even know they are there?

Breakfast Options

Pancakes

Bad: Pancakes made with regular pancake mix, eggs, vegetable oil, and regular syrup.

Good: Pancakes made with whole-wheat pancake mix, egg whites, and sugar-free syrup. (Note: pancakes made with regular pancake mix and sugar-free syrup is a *major* improvement over pancakes with regular syrup)

Scrambled Eggs, Bacon, and Sausage

Bad: Four eggs scrambled with regular cheese, regular bacon, and regular sausage.

Good: Two eggs and three egg whites scrambled with shredded fat-free cheese, 50 percent less-fat bacon or turkey bacon, light sausage or turkey sausage.

Cereal and Toast

Bad: High-sugar cereal with 2 percent or whole milk and two pieces of toast with made with regular bread and jelly or butter.

Good: High-fiber or low-sugar cereal with skim milk and two pieces of light wheat toast with sugar free jelly or fat free spray butter.

Bacon, Egg, and Cheese Sandwich or Biscuit

Bad: Two eggs scrambled, regular bacon, and regular cheese on regular bread or a biscuit.

Good: One egg and two egg whites scrambled with 50 percent less-fat bacon or turkey bacon and 2 percent cheese on light wheat bread

The above items are just a few of many, many meal options. The key is to learn the principles and acquire the ability to take any meal that would fall into the "bad" category and apply those principles to make changes to that meal so that it would fall into the "good" category. These are all good options, and some of them are better than others, but they are not all the healthiest options that you will find. Remember, since it is all relative to what *you* normally do, and since all we are trying to do is *improve* what *you* normally do, then ultimately what makes a meal a "good" meal is not how good it really is, but rather, how much better it is than what you regularly do. If you normally eat greasy bacon double cheeseburgers, then you could actually improve by eating greasy cheeseburgers without bacon. It is all about progression. You eliminate that bacon on the cheeseburger, then later on, switch to a grilled chicken sandwich, and so on. There are many healthy options available to you. Your goal should be to choose more and more of them as you progress throughout time. The problem is that most people read about a certain strict diet or see some health-freak that they want to look like and try to follow their strict, miserable diets, and then they fail. **YOU ARE NOT GOING TO GET YOUR RESULTS IN THIRTY DAYS**, so don't eat as if you are. Look at the big picture. Plan on steady, progressive improvements. You will last longer and have better and more permanent results. *Eat strict enough to get results, but not so strict that you quit!*

CHAPTER SEVEN

Eating Healthy – The Healing Power of Fruits and Vegetables

Most of the nutrition and food talk so far has been aimed at calorie reduction and losing body fat, which are areas that lead to a leaner and healthier you. Another very important aspect to dieting is eating for your health—eating fruits and vegetables. The health benefits of eating large amounts of fruits and vegetables are incredible. Study after study shows that eating seven to ten servings of raw fruits and vegetables each day can drastically decrease your chances of heart disease, stroke, type-2 diabetes, and even cancer. Fruits and vegetables can provide great improvement to your immune system, your joint health, your mental clarity, and long list of many more great benefits. However, people run into many problems when it comes to fruits and vegetables. Fruit can be fattening, yet people will eat tons of it because it is good for them. A glass of orange juice has many wonderful nutrient qualities, like vitamin C, but it is very fattening and can lead to weight gain, which can lead to many other health problems. Vegetables are rarely eaten raw, which is when their nutrient content is the best, and often, vegetables are cooked and then loaded with grease, salt, and butter.

With fruits and vegetables, there has to be balance. Often, people use fruits and vegetables as a crutch. People will think, "it's fruit; it's healthy; I can eat as much as I want," and they will eat bowl after bowl of fruit each and every night as a snack and to get nutritional benefits, but what they really get is a lot of extra calories and sugar, which can lead to weight gain and potential health problems. The negative of the extra calories, if eaten in excess, can actually outweigh the benefits of fruit. Remember, though, it's all relevant, so if you switch from a bowl of ice cream each night to a bowl of fruit salad, then you are making a great improvement in both calories and nutrition. What I am mostly referring to are the people who give themselves the green light to eat as much fruit as they want because it is fruit—and fruit is good for you. The same can be said for vegetables. I hear all the time; "Oh, I eat good, I eat vegetables all the time." What they are really telling me is that they go to a meat-n-three restaurant every day and get a fatty meat and three vegetables, which are all either fried or soaked in butter. In this situation, most of the nutrients of the vegetables have been cooked out of them and the butter and/or grease has now turned a healthy vegetable into a very fattening and unhealthy food. People also think that they are eating healthy when they are eating vegetables, but then they load them up with salt. However, the salt dangers outweigh the positives of the vegetables.

Don't take my advice on fruits and vegetables the wrong way. I *do* recommend eating fruits and vegetables. I just wanted to point out how they can be used in the wrong way.

As mentioned before, countless studies have shown the wonderful health benefits of fruits and vegetables, especially raw fruits and vegetables, which have the highest nutrient levels. It is OK to eat cooked vegetables, because, like stated before, it is still good for you and it is *definitely* better for you than not eating vegetables and not getting any nutrients. The same is true for fruit; fruit is good for you, especially when it takes the place of something that is bad for you, like high-sugar sweets.

You do need fruits and vegetables and you need to have a good balance of them in your diet. You need seven to thirteen servings of raw fruits and vegetables per day to reap the benefits! The problem is that it is nearly impossible to eat that many fruits and vegetables per day. It would cost way too much and it would put your calorie totals way too high. I still try to incorporate fruits and vegetables into my diet, as much as I can while still being where I want to be in terms of calories. Vitamin supplements can help a little, but they only provide a small fraction of what you need, and most of what is in a vitamin isn't even absorbed into the body. (Actually, there are studies out there that show that some vitamin supplements provide little-to-no help at all, and in some ways can have adverse effects on your health.) Raw fruits and vegetables are the best way to get your nutrients, but also the most inconvenient way! I take fruit and vegetable capsules every day to ensure that I am getting my appropriate fruit and vegetable nutrients without excess calories. The capsules, filled with seventeen servings of organically-grown raw fruits and vegetables, are absorbed straight into the blood stream, unlike vitamins that have to be carried in with food. These are not multi-vitamins; they are ***whole food nutrition.*** The capsules retain the nutrient content of the fruits and vegetables through a juicing process and they contain only a few calories. They are the perfect way for me to get my nutrients and not ruin my calories. I still eat a lot of fruits and vegetables, but these capsules basically give me an insurance policy on my nutrition. It is literally $15 dollars worth of fruits and vegetables per day for about $1.50. To learn more about the fruits and vegetable capsules that I take, email me at info@hooverfitness.com and I will send you information on the product.

CHAPTER EIGHT

Diet Cheat Sheet

Sometimes changes are easier to make when you put them on paper. Take some time and complete the following sheet. Read labels and do some research to find the less-calorie options. This will help you reduce your daily caloric intake by reducing each item that you normally eat.

On the left side, write down anything that you normally eat. On the right side, write down an option that you will enjoy as much, or almost as much, that has fewer calories. You will now have a lower calorie replacement for everything that you eat—*except for your cheat meals*!

Normal Foods I Eat	Less-Calorie Option
1.	1.
2.	2.
3.	3.
4.	4.
5.	5.
6.	6.
7.	7.
8.	8.
9.	9.
10.	10.

11.	11.
12.	12.
13.	13.
14.	14.
15.	15.

V.
EXERCISE – *TIME TO START MOVING*

CHAPTER ONE

Introduction

We have discussed the importance of taking care of your self. We have discussed how to approach health from a mental perspective. We have discussed how to eat better. Now it is time to learn about exercise. Your "situation" is your diet, cardio, and weight training. You cannot achieve results without improving your situation. The diet can be changed and you can get results, but to maximize even more results, you need to improve the cardio and exercise portions of your situation.

Most people tend to take one of two different paths; they just go on a diet and get some results, or they exercise like crazy and never improve their diet. You can get results from either way, but to maximize your results, you need to improve your diet, cardio, and weights at the same time. That being said, how much you decide to improve each one can vary. You can improve your diet a little and your exercise a lot or improve your exercise a little and your diet a lot. In the beginning, do what is easiest for you, then over time, work on improving everything. The bottom line is, to be in good shape you have to eat better, do cardio, and lift weights. If you think, "I don't need to work out," or "I don't have to do cardio," you couldn't be more wrong. Take a look at the people that are in good shape that you would like to look like and I guarantee to you that they lift weights and do cardio.

CHAPTER TWO

History and Trends

For centuries, humans have exercised and enjoyed the benefits. Throughout history, the most active people have always looked the best and been the healthiest. The human body is designed to be a work in progress. You have to mold and shape it constantly. You have to take care of it constantly. It has always been that way and it will always be.

Instead of going throughout all of human history and studying what primitive man did, we will look at the trends of the last fifty years or so and learn from them to shape the future of exercise.

Weight training really started to blossom in the in the 50s and 60s. People started working out with weights and developing routines based on core exercises like pull ups, push ups, squats, and others. People also began running more as a form of exercise and athletic training. By the 1970s, weight training had made the big time. Health clubs were opening up everywhere, bodybuilding was gaining notoriety, and the emergence of weight machines was really starting to take off. Cardiovascular exercise was growing, from running to the addition of aerobics classes. The 1980s brought us the mega health clubs and introduced going to the gym as a "social experience." The good thing that emerged was that more people were going to health clubs and exercising more. Weight training was a good mixture of free weight exercises and machine exercise. Cardiovascular training was now based mostly on three different areas: classes, treadmills, and exercise bikes. Group classes really took off in the 80s. In the 1990s, the growth continued. Weight training evolved even more, classes continued to grow, and more and more health clubs opened. The 90s brought us better, more user-friendly weight training machines. The 90s also saw the emergence of the stair stepper, the elliptical, and the birth of group cycling classes. From the 90s to present day, weight training, cardio, and group classes have continued to grow. In the 2000s, the traditional exercises have remained, but the addition of functional training, quick fad-type programs, yoga, pilates, sports-specific training, boot camps, and workout videos have all played a part in broadening our exercise horizons. They have also hindered our results to some degree. People wanted what they wanted when they wanted it and this attitude carried over into exercising as we entered the 2000s. Get-results-quick programs took over; and like fad diets, the results, if any, were short lived. Two lessons emerged from the growth of options in exercise. First, the new, fun, different programs are good, when done in addition to traditional programs, or when used as a get-off-the-couch motivator and for accountability purposes. Second, the traditional core exercises are still great for results!

The importance of exercise has continued to grow in society. People have learned that they have to take care of themselves. What has history taught us? Basically, that exercise is important. You can't replace working hard with a fad-workout; the traditional exercises are tried and true, and the spectrum of choices such as traditional workouts, functional workouts, various cardio equipment, numerous group classes, and accountability can all be used together to consistently achieve results.

CHAPTER THREE

No More Excuses – Make Exercise a Habit

Do you want to look better, feel better, and be a healthier person? Do you *really* want to? Then you have to make exercise a habit—NO MORE EXCUSES. It's easy to come up with reasons why not to exercise and diet. Instead of focusing on the "why not," we should focus on the "why." Want three reasons why? You will look better, feel better, and be healthier. Want more? You will live longer, look younger, save money, relieve stress, sleep better, have more quality time with your kids, etcetera, etcetera, the list just keeps going. To prevent health problems, you have to take care of yourself. You have to take preventative measures, which means that you have to eat better and exercise. There is no other way. You may tell yourself that there is another way, but deep down, you know it is just an excuse and you are just delaying the inevitable. But, if you delay too long, there could be major consequences.

I have heard just about every excuse imaginable when it comes to reasons not to exercise. Some common "why not" excuses include:

"I don't have time to exercise" – You may be very busy and struggle to have time to do things, but the truth is, you *will* make time to do the things that are important to you.

Also, if you don't take care of yourself, then you will have to *make* time for health problems. Health problems don't care what your time restraints are.

"I can't afford a gym membership" – Times are tough and pennies need to be saved. Like the time excuse, you will find a way to pay for the things that are important to you. For a monthly cost that is cheaper than a trip to the movies or a round of golf, it *can* be afforded. Think about it. Can you not afford it, or are you just using financial restraints as an "out" to having to exercise. Can you really put a dollar figure on your health?

"My doctor told me not to exercise" – Did your doctor really tell you *not* to exercise? If so, then fire him!! Doctors are here to help you get well. (Exercise is to help you not have to go to the doctor.) No matter what your ailment is, there is a form of exercise that can benefit you. Once again, if you don't exercise, then you have accepted your ailment and whatever implications come with it.

"I'm just too tired to exercise after work" – If you take a week or two and ignore those tired feelings and start exercising, you will feel better. The more you exercise, the more energy you have and the better you sleep, thus, the better you will feel on a daily basis. Tough it out at first and it will get better.

"I'm too old to get in shape, it's too late" – It is never too late to be in better shape. No matter where you are in life, if you take better care of yourself, you will have a better quality of life for the remainder of your life, no matter how long that may be.

Make exercise a habit. You don't have to exercise until you puke or pass out. You just need to make it a part of your life. The reality is, if we want to look good, feel good, and be healthy, then we have to make exercising a higher priority in our lives. *Laziness is a disease, but it's curable!*

You need to find motivation. Without motivation, exercise seems useless. It seems like a dead-end street. If you have no motivation, then you have no reason *why*.

Find your motivation before it finds you.

Start thinking of reasons why you should take care of yourself. Is it to prevent health problems? Is it to fell better? Is it to look better? Is it to be more active with your kids? Is it to be better at a sport? There are many reasons why. What you don't want to happen is a reason find you— like being diagnosed with diabetes or having a heart attack. If you get diabetes, you will be motivated to take care of yourself to prevent future problems. If you have a heart attack, you will have to exercise to stay alive. In these and many other situations, the motivation found you. That is not the way it should be. In the beginning, search for and find your motivation, and remind yourself of it daily. It could be as simple as a picture hanging on your mirror as a daily reminder of how you want to look. It could be a name printed on your planner of a friend or relative that had complications from health problems. It could be your children. The list could go on forever. Use your motivation to achieve results, and then those results will provide the motivation from then on. You will not want to lose the results that you achieved. Most people quit before this point, so find a motivation and tough it out until you get results, and then it can be smooth sailing from there!

CHAPTER FOUR

Improve *Your* routine – *A Progressive Approach*

Just like diet, exercise should be approached in a progressive way. Too often, people will try an extremely difficult or intense exercise routine that is too many levels above their current routine (which many times is not a routine at all). It is all relative to what *you* are currently doing. To improve *your* body, you must improve *your* exercise routine. Failure usually occurs when people go from not working out at all to trying some all-out, super-intense program. They are miserable, can't handle it, and quit. The good news is that you *can* achieve any results that you want. The bad news is that in order to do it right and actually achieve those results, it takes some time. Results are achieved constantly on an ongoing basis. Slower results are easier to achieve and easier to maintain. The only requirement is patience.

See the big picture.

Exercise is not something that you can start, work for three months, get your results, and then quit. It is a life-long process. Exercise has to be a part of your life if you want to look good and feel good. Your body needs exercise like it needs food, water, oxygen, nutrients, sunlight, sleep, and anything else essential for life. Your body is like a car. It needs regular maintenance if it is going to run well. Our bodies are designed to be taken care of and exercise is part of the plan! It is really scary how many people don't realize this. You have to see the big picture. The big picture is the results that you will achieve in the long run. If you exercise on a progressive, always improving, lifelong basis, then you will see results for a long time. Your goal should not be to achieve your ultimate goal in only one or two months. Your goal should be to make a positive change in one or two months, another improvement one or two months later, and on and on for a long time.

Take progressive steps in improving your exercise. To get results, you only need to go to the level above where you currently are. If you don't exercise at all, then you are at level zero. You will see results by starting with level one. Level one for someone that does not exercise could be getting off the couch and walking thirty minutes every other day. That is *very easy*, but since it is more work than sitting on the couch, then that person, who usually sits on the couch and does not exercise, will see results. Now those results will slow or stop after a certain period of time. When that happens, then it is time to go to level two. Level two may be jogging or adding an easy weight routine. What each level is for each person is different. What determines the next level is what your current level is. Take a look at what you currently do and find an easy way to improve it. Make that one improvement and you will see results. When the results slow, then improve that routine, and so on. Take the steps; go from one step to the next.

Don't jump too many steps.

Take small steps. So, it may take you longer...big deal. It will be easier. You will get better results—results that will last longer. You will be less likely to burn out this way. People try to jump in too fast when they want to improve their exercise. They see someone in a magazine or they hear what their favorite television star is doing and they try to do what that person does. They end up over-working. They become miserable. They quit. That situation is a failure from the beginning. Chances are, that person on the cover of the magazine didn't go from doing nothing to doing the routine that they are currently doing. They developed their routine over time. Results are progressive!

Work hard enough to get results, but not so hard that you quit.

Logically and progressively approach exercise. Yes, you do have to work hard to get results, but the good news is that you only have to work harder than you previously were working in order to get results. If you are not getting results, then take a look at your routine and find a way to improve it. Take your routine to the next level.

85

CHAPTER FIVE

Weight Training – *Everybody Needs It*

Weight training is an important part of your regimen. Often neglected, lifting weights is a necessity for everyone. No matter who you are, you need to workout with weights. There are several benefits of weight training, including strength, muscle development, increased boned density, and increased metabolism. After age forty, the average person begins to lose muscle mass each year. That loss of muscle mass can be combated with weight training.

When you lift weights, you gain *strength*. When you become stronger, everything becomes easier. Your quality of life improves. When you are stronger, you get injured less. Stronger muscles means less burden on your joints, which means that you can actually improve joint pain, or possibly prevent joint injuries by weight training. When you are stronger, everything from walking up stairs and cleaning the house to lifting boxes and mowing the lawn becomes easier.

A second benefit of weight training is *muscle development* and symmetry. When you do cardiovascular exercise, you burn body fat, when you lift weights, you build muscles. Muscles are what shape your body. You can't be *in shape* without muscles. Body fat just lays there and has no shape. Muscles are attached to the joints and pulled tight to provide shape. Don't forget, to see the shape of the muscle, you have to burn the body fat that is covering them.

A third, and possibly most important benefit of weight training, is *increased bone density*. Osteoporosis is a bone density disease that affects men and women. More than twenty-eight million Americans have osteoporosis or are at risk of developing it. Countless studies have shown that weight training can drastically decrease the chances of acquiring osteoporosis and actually, in some cases, can reverse osteoporosis in people who already have it. "Weight-bearing" and "load-bearing" exercise help keep bones strong by causing the muscles and tendons to pull on the bones, which in turn stimulates bone cells to produce more bone. Just as muscle gets stronger and bigger the more you use it, a bone becomes stronger and denser when you place demands on it. Weight training is the overall best way to exercise to increase your bone density.

The last benefit of weight training that we will look at is *increased metabolism*. (Although, there are many more benefits to weight training than the four mentioned here.) You have two major forces at work when it comes to exercising—body fat and muscle. Your body contains a lot of both. You want less body fat and more muscle. Muscle burns more calories than fat does. When you do cardio, your body burns calories during the exercise and burns body fat during the exercise. When you finish your cardio, your body doesn't continue to burn calories as it did during the exercise. When you lift weights, you burn calories and you build muscle. The more muscle that you have in your body, the more calories it will burn throughout the day. So, weight lifting not only burns calories throughout the workout, it can help you burn body fat when you are not working out by increasing your metabolism. Get in the weight room and build some muscle. Turn your body into a twenty-four-seven calorie-burning machine!

Ladies – You won't "get big" if you workout.

Women will not "get big" if they workout with weights. I battle with women on a daily basis trying to prove to them that they will not get bigger by working out. Take a look at the fifteen most-fit bodies that you know of. I guarantee to you that they lift weights. That should be enough proof, but I will explain further. As females, your body does not produce muscle as easily as men (Estrogen vs. Testosterone). This is why, in general, men are bigger and more muscular than women. If a female wants to gain mass, she has to work twice as hard in the weight room and totally gear her diet for mass and growth. *And she still will have trouble gaining size!* What about the female body-builders—the very big, guy-looking ones? Well, chances are, they supplemented with male hormones to gain that muscle, which can also explain how their voices and other features begin to show male characteristics. "But, I *did* lift weights when I was younger and *I did* get bigger." What probably happened was that since you were younger, what little muscle-building ability your body had was increased, and you also did not do anything to burn the body fat on top of the muscle. Basically, you gained a nice amount of lean muscle, maybe a quarter of an inch increase, but since you didn't burn any body fat (cardio and diet), all that you did was push the fat up! You still have to eat better and do cardio, but if you do those things and lift weights, you will burn body fat and build lean muscle, thus improving your "shape," not your "size." You may actually burn one and a half inches of body fat and gain a half of an inch of muscle, which would mean that you lost an inch of size and improved your shape at the same time! If you just do cardio and diet, as many females do, then you will just get *skinny.* If you want to look better and have curves and shape, then you need to lift weights also.

Male or female – Do we workout differently?

Surprisingly, men and women should not work very differently. Many times, we see men working out a certain way and women doing things another way. Usually, the women do lighter, less impact exercises, because of the fear of getting big like a man by doing "guy exercises." That is a myth. The traditional, effective, weight lifting exercises are great for men and women. Your growth is determined more by your diet and how much you lift, than by which exercises that you do. Again, women, take a look at some of the more fit females that you see, and chances are, they are working out like men, or like what one might think a "guy" workout is. I am not saying that a woman has to be a meathead in the weight room and just do bench presses and dead-lifts. What I am saying is not to neglect certain exercises because you think that they are for men. Don't use that thinking as a crutch or an excuse not to work hard. In my experience as a personal trainer, I have trained men and women with mostly the same exercises. I usually just adjust reps and weight or amount of certain exercises based on individual goals, which are usually different for males and females.

Men – If you want to grow, lift hard and eat for growth.

I have spent the last few paragraphs talking about how difficult it is for women to gain size. It is also difficult for men to gain muscle. If you want to only lean up, then work out a lot and do a lot of cardio. If growth is your primary goal, then you need to lift as heavy as you can, stick to most-ly big-muscle-group exercises like chest, back, and legs, and you have to eat a ton of protein. To grow, you probably will have to eat a lot more than you are used to, a lot more than you think. You also need to give your body time to recover, because growth takes place during rest and recovery. When you lift weights, you break down your muscles, and then they recover. They recover bigger and stronger each time. How much bigger and stronger is determined by how much you lift and how you are eating. You want to work every muscle in your body, but for growth, place the most importance on large muscle groups and on diet.

Reps determine heavy or light, not weight.

People hear that if they lift a light weight and do high rep-etitions, then they will become toned and not put on any bulk. So, they use very light weight and do easy sets of twenty or more reps, and never get any results! That is because they are not working hard. To tone your body, pick a higher rep range, like fifteen reps. *Then lift as heavy as you can fifteen times.* If you can do it twenty five times, then it is way too light. If you can only do it four times, then it is too heavy. The amount of times that you can lift determines if it is heavy or not, not the actual weight. Do you want to tone? Then pick a rep range between twelve and eighteen. Do you want to build? Then pick a rep range between four and eight reps. Work as hard as you can in your rep range. Remember, *weight is just a number!*

Cheat some to work hard.

Strict form is not good. You can't have strict form and work hard enough to overload your muscles. Your muscles respond to muscle overload and hard work. Strict form doesn't allow this. On the flip side, bad form is unsafe. You need to be in the middle. Don't be too strict, but don't be unsafe. You need to cheat a little to lift more weight and do more reps, but not so much that it is unsafe—just enough to work hard. It is what I call an "effective cheat." Use your body to create a little momentum to lift more or get some extra reps. As long as your form has not altered the exercise or changed the muscles involved, then the "cheat" is good. An example of this is standing straight bar arm curls: You can lean a little forward at the bottom of the repetition and sway back to upright when you are curling to get a little momentum. Your arms do the EXACT same movement as they would with strict form. You just created a little momentum to get a few extra reps or do a little more weight. Don't start your curls in an upright position and then, when you start to struggle, lean back and cheat by stressing your back, going from upright to bending your lower back. In the "effective cheat," you went from slightly bent over to upright. In the unsafe example, you went from upright to bent back, with a lot of stress on the lower back. In the unsafe example, you got halfway through the rep and then it got too tough, so you used your back. In the safe cheat, your previous rep indicated that you might need help on the next rep, so you prepared for a struggle and did the entire rep based on needing a little help. It is basically a "self-spot." I am not saying use momentum on every rep, but do use it on heavy weights or extra reps to allow yourself to work a little harder. You can do strict form for eight reps then stop, or you can do strict form for eight reps and then cheat a little to get two or three more reps. The first eight reps were the same, but you got two or three more reps by safely cheating a little. Eight great plus two good is better than eight great and zero good!

Prioritize your exercises.

Another key element of weight training is to prioritize your exercises during each workout. When you start working out, you have a full energy tank. You will get the most out of the exercises that you do when you have the most energy. Later in the workout, when you are tired, the effectiveness drops some. Prioritize the exercises that you do. Do bigger body parts before smaller ones. Do more effective exercises before less effective ones. An example is working your chest before your triceps. When you work your chest, you are working your triceps. The opposite is not always true. You want a great chest workout and your arms will develop just from working your chest. Your chest will not develop just from working your triceps. You don't want to do triceps pushdowns, wear out your triceps, then try to do your chest workout. Do your chest workout first then use whatever energy you have left over to work your triceps. The same holds true for back and biceps. Your biceps will grow just from working out your back. You still need to work your biceps, but work your back first. To break it down further, within a chest workout, presses are much more effective than flies, so do your presses first, when you have the most energy, and do your flies after the presses. What about super-setting and going back and forth? I am a big fan of switching from exercise to exercise. Just go from big body part to big body part or from small body part to small body part or from upper body to lower body. Examples are super-setting chest exercises with other chest exercises or super-setting chest with back our supper-setting legs and arms, as opposed to super-setting chest and arms. There are many, many, ways to workout. I am going to explain the ways that I think are the most effective. There are many combinations of body parts to work together and there are even total-body workouts. It is hard to go wrong as long as you are doing *something*. The more serious you want to get into developing your body, the more you might want to strategize which workouts that you do. The workout plans given later in the book will break down different body-part splits. The bottom line is, if you workout hard and consistently, you will get results, no matter what you do!

With so many different ways to workout, what should I do?

   In this section, we will look at certain "types" of workouts. Later in the book, I will show you specific workouts. There are many different ways to workout, but the two main ways that we will focus on are **traditional** workouts and **functional** workouts.

   Traditional weight training is tried and true and very effective. Functional training has gained a lot of popularity in recent years and can be very effective as well. Traditional weight training consists of exercises like free weights and weight training machines. Most of the movements in traditional exercises are done in a specific position that requires certain joint movements in only one direction, thus working specific muscles or muscle groups. The main advantage to this traditional working out is that it is the *best* way to build and shape muscles. Traditional weight training is a relatively safe way to workout because your joints are usually fixed and operate in a stable position. Traditional weight training is great for developing strength and power, and improving your body's shape.

Functional training is very popular also. Functional training involves many different movements in many different directions, often including several muscle groups at one time. The main advantage to functional training is that these exercises are different, thus eliminating boredom. Functional training is also great for improving athletic ability.

If you are an athlete and you only do traditional exercise, you will still need to work on you athletic movements. Contrarily, if you only do functional exercise, you will improve only your athletic ability and your strength and looks may not improve unless you can incorporate traditional exercise. You need to exercise both ways. Many people can be all-or-nothing when it comes to working out. "My way or the highway" type of thinking. Be more open minded. Why not get the best of both worlds. Both styles of working out are effective. I see people all the time who only do traditional weight training and look great, but cannot perform athletically at all. I also see people that only do functional training because they heard it was the new, most effective way to workout and they think that traditional working out is a thing of the past. These people often work hard, feel better, and improve their athletic ability, but these people usually don't look quite the way they would like. The bottom line is the fact that it is all relative to what *you* do. If you are not exercising at all and you start a functional program, you will get results. I recommend that you mix it up and do a little of both. Take the advantages of both traditional and functional exercises. Do a majority of traditional exercises, but also include some functional movements in your routine as well, or do a few days of traditional and a few days of functional each week. Nothing says you can't do both! If both have benefits, why not train both ways? There is no law saying that you have to pick just one. I personally, think that traditional exercises are the best because you get stronger and can look incredible, but I also like doing functional work because I like to keep my athletic ability improving as well. Other people like the functional work because it is different and exciting. Both ways are effective. Be open minded. Below are some examples of traditional exercises and functional exercises:

<u>Traditional</u>
Bench Press
Dumbbell Press
Chest Fly
Lat Pull-downs
Seated Row
Shoulder Press
Arm Curls
Triceps Extensions
Squats
Leg Extensions
Leg Curls
Leg Press
Weight Machines

<u>Functional Exercises</u>
Kettle Bell Exercises
Medicine Ball Exercises
Plyometric Exercises
Push Ups and Pull Ups
Box Jumps

Grass Drills
Ball Exercises
Band Exercises
Jumping Jacks

Another way in which people like to train is called "sports-specific" training. This type of training is when an athlete will perform specific exercises that are targeted at helping him/her at their specific sport. This is very popular for teenagers trying to compete in specific sports or adults trying to exercise for their golf game. Most sports-specific trainers will only train those "specific" exercises for that sport. The athlete will improve some, but eventually the results can slow down. To me, training sports-specific only is a narrow-minded approach. Why not do it all? I train my athletes with a more well-rounded approach, no matter what their specific sport is. If they never do traditional exercises, they will have trouble gaining strength to apply to improving their sport movements. It is hard to make the same muscles jump higher and run faster without strengthening those muscles. We strengthen them with traditional exercises. Teaching young athletes a combination of sports-specific and traditional exercises will not only help their sport, it will also teach them the fundamentals of weight training that they can use for the rest of their life, when sports are no longer a part of it. For athletes, we work traditionally some, but we also incorporate functional exercises and specific sports movements. The traditional work gets them ready to train for their sport. Every athlete should improve in three areas, which are traditional working out, sports-specific exercises, and skills practice for their particular sport. Too often, people only do one or two of the three areas. Be the best, do all three!

Just remember that the fundamental core exercises are great for everyone, no matter what your goals are. There should never be a time in someone's life where chest presses, squats, leg presses, pull-downs, rows, military presses, triceps pushdowns, arm curls, back extensions, and sit-ups are not a part of your routine. If you are training for something specific, then do these exercises *and* your "specific" exercises. The specific stuff will come and go, sports will come and go, ninety day this-and-that will come and go, but these core exercises arc tried and true.

Stop doing so many crunches!

Good news for those of you who want a six-pack—*you don't have to do so many ab exercises to get a six-pack!* Stop doing so many crunches. Crunches can be easy and if you are doing hundreds per day, then you are wasting valuable time. The days of hundreds of crunches are over. Abdominal exercises are important, and you do need to work your abs regularly, but the way to a six-pack is not hours and hours of ab work. You need to do some ab work, but your abs will develop by doing a variety of ab exercises and by doing other exercises as well. If you are working hard enough, no matter what exercise you are doing, you will engage your abs. Another key factor to look at is body fat. You can have the best abdominal muscles in the world, but if you do nothing to burn the body fat laying over those muscles, then you will never see them. When I want more of a six-pack, I eat better and do more cardio. Basically, I burn the body fat on top of my ab muscles. I am not saying to quit doing ab exercises, I am saying that you should do some ab work and then focus the extra time and energy on more cardio or more effective weight-training exercises. **It is a mental shift.** Most people have spent the majority of their life thinking that if they don't do a certain amount of reps for their abs, then they will not have a flat stomach. Mentally you may think that you are not going to get a flat stomach this way, but trust me, you will. **Reverse your thinking.** I am asked just about every day, "What machine will give me a flat tummy?" and I always point to the treadmill!

Stretch before? Stretch After? Stretch at all?

Should I stretch before I exercise, after I exercise, or should I even stretch at all? Stretching is a confusing subject. You will hear a different answer about stretching from just about anyone that you ask. My opinion is, like everything else, don't neglect it and keep it simple. You don't have to waste your time with thirty-minute stretch sessions, but you do need to do some stretching. My professional suggestion is to lightly stretch or "loosen-up" before cardio or weight training. Maybe stretch for about a minute or two. This is really to get the blood flowing and the muscles ready to work. It is important not to over-stretch before exercise and tire out the muscle, thus resulting in a poor workout. During the workout, if you feel tight after a set, lightly stretch some to keep the blood flowing and the muscles from cramping. After cardio or weight training, I recommend some more stretching. Maybe five minutes total, and stretch everything, especially the areas that were just worked the most. Stretching will help with reducing soreness. Stretch through the soreness when muscles are sore. This will help alleviate pain and reduce soreness. Stretching will also improve circulation, lengthen your muscles, improve your flexibility, and help prevent injury. If you stretch regularly, you will stay flexible; and the more flexible you are, the more effective you will be at sports and athletic movements and the less injury-prone you will be. Stretched muscles are "ready" for whatever movements you place on them. Un-stretched, tight muscles get pulled or injured more easily. Incorporate stretching into your routine and you will feel the benefits.

Exercise, rest, recover, repeat.

There are benefits to rest and recovery. When you workout, you break your muscles down. Basically, you are tearing them apart. When you rest, those muscles recover. When a muscle recovers, it recovers bigger and stronger. The more often you work a muscle, the more it stays broken-down. There are different levels of rest and recovery. A bodybuilder, or someone who just wants to grow as much as possible needs to lift each muscle group a great amount and let each muscle group recover for a longer amount of time. If you are working hard enough on each muscle, you can work them once per week and let them recover for a week. The opposite end of the spectrum is working every body part every day. This is very effective for getting in better shape, conditioning muscles, and improving muscle endurance. It is more difficult to grow by working each muscle every day, but if growth is not your goal, then this can be effective. An effective balance of work and rest is to give each body part one to three days recovery and then work them again. This gives the muscles enough time to recover, but not so much time that they become dormant. Remember, the more exercise the better, but don't forget to rest some. Give your muscles a break. Tired muscles are more prone to injury. Fresh muscles will work harder. You need to rest physically *and* mentally. Don't exercise every single day. Once a week or so, give yourself a break. Let your energy recover and your motivation as well.

CHAPTER SIX

Get Up and Get Moving –
The Importance of Cardio

Cardiovascular training (aka cardio or aerobic training), is one of the most beneficial things that you can do for your body. Cardio can be defined as any exercise that elevates your heart rate, and keeps it consistently elevated for fifteen minutes or longer. The opposite is anaerobic training, which is what weight training and sprinting are. Anaerobic training is elevating your heart rate very high, then resting, then repeating. Anaerobic training is great for strength, speed, and muscle building. Cardio training is great for burning calories and burning body fat. Cardio is great for your heart. Cardio increases your heart rate and helps your heart become healthier and function better. Another great benefit from cardio is increased endurance. You will be able to last longer and go further with your exercise, sports, or anything that requires energy in your daily life. Cardiovascular training can increase your lung capacity. When you do cardiovascular training, you breathe more and you breathe deeper, and your lungs fill up with oxygen and expand. Constant breathing and expansion helps increase your lung capacity.

You need a well-rounded program, which is weight training, cardio, and diet. You have to do all three. It is very difficult to get lean and burn body fat without doing cardio.

Think of it like this: Weight training is for strength and muscle, cardio is to burn body fat, and your diet is for both. If you do cardio consistently, you will look better, feel better, and improve your overall health.

You can't sweat it off if you don't sweat.

Intensity is the name of the game when it comes to cardio. If you want to see results, then you have to work hard. I hear all the time, "I do cardio, I walk my dog every night." My response is always, "No, you don't do cardio, you walk your dog." Remember, hard work is relevant you. Hard work may be walking your dog, but for most people, hard work is much more than that. If you go from the couch to walking around the block, you will see results, but eventually, the results will slow; then you have to go from walking around the block to jogging or something else more difficult. Don't lie to yourself! People will justify certain activities as cardio to make themselves feel better, but they never see results. If you want to see results, you have to work hard.

It's not how long you go or how far you go, it's how hard you work.

It is better to work hard for thirty minutes than it is to work easy for an hour. Don't get into the thinking of, "I have to go an hour" or "I have to go three miles." It is not how long you go or how far you go. It is *how hard you work*. Chances are that you are using those time or distance markers as a barrier to working hard. If you can make it an hour, you probably are not working hard enough. You *will* get better results by working hard. I am not saying that you have to work so hard that you pass out or that you only make it ten minutes. What I am saying is that you don't have to do an hour; you can get results in thirty minutes. I am saying that you should work hard. People want results without the work. (So do I!) The reality is that we have to work hard to get results.

"My arms are toning, but I can't seem to lose in other areas."

When you weight train, you build muscle, and you can target specific muscles and work them. Body fat is a little different. When you burn body fat, you burn the same amount everywhere, but when you gain body fat, you gain in some areas more than others. People would like to do what is called "spot-reducing," which means that they would like to work an area and lose only in that particular area. Unfortunately, spot-reducing is not possible. You burn body fat through cardio, calorie deficit, and increased metabolism. And when you burn body fat, you lose it everywhere. If it seems like you can't lose in a certain area, don't get discouraged. You *are* losing in that area. Be patient. The following example may help understand the process. Let's say that you have one inch of fat in your arms and four inches in your stomach area. You then proceed to do cardio and eat better. You end up losing one inch of body fat. Your arm went from one inch of fat to zero. Your stomach went from four inches to three. When you look at your arm, you see a lean arm. When you look at your stomach, you still see three inches of fat. So, your thinking is that you can't lose the body fat in your stomach because you still see fat there. Be patient, because when you work hard again for another period of time, you will burn another inch. Your arm will stay at zero inches of body fat, but your stomach will go from three inches to two. This process can go on and on until you lose body fat everywhere. The areas in which you have the most fat take longer to become lean because there is more there to lose. Be patient, you *can* lose everywhere.

Change it up for maximum results.

With cardio training, more so than weight training, people seem to do the same thing over and over. Doing the same routine over and over is good for consistency and for just being active, but if you really want to see results, then you need to change things up. Do you do the same speed for the same time on the treadmill every day? Do you do the same thirty-minute elliptical routine every day? Do you do the same bike program every day? Chances are, if you do the same thing every day, it has become easy, and if it is easy, then you will not get results. The *same* thing produces the *same* results. We don't want the same results; we want different results…better results. Step out of the norm and change it up. Try a progressive routine on a machine. Start at a medium level and increase the resistance every minute or two. This will help you keep your heart rate elevated as you get more used to the workout. Interval training is another good way to change it up. Be careful, as there is one possible pitfall with interval training, which is too much rest between intervals. Remember, during cardio, the heart rate needs to stay elevated, so if you rest too long between intervals, you could fall into anaerobic training. You can also try mixing different machines together to change up your cardio routine. If you want to do thirty minutes of cardio, try ten intensity-packed minutes on three different machines. This is a very effective way to get in thirty great minutes. It is easier to work hard for ten minutes three different times than to work hard for thirty minutes one time. Just remember to go from one machine to the next without resting. Changing up your cardio routine will help you fight boredom and make you work harder, thus help you get better results!

YOU need cardio training.

Do yourself a favor and start doing cardio. Your heart will thank you. You will look better, feel better, sleep better, have more energy, have more endurance, and gain many more benefits. Don't talk yourself out of doing cardio, make a commitment to get up and get moving. *Everyone* has to do cardio to see results. Get started today. Make a commitment for a positive change in your life!

CHAPTER SEVEN

Stand Up Straight – The Importance of Good Posture and it's Effects on the Body

One of the worst habits you can have is practicing bad posture. Bad posture not only looks bad, but it also affects your entire body and the way it feels and performs. Start practicing better posture and you will look better, feel better, become stronger, and reduce the risks of back and other injuries.

If you have poor posture, your bones are not properly aligned and your joints and ligaments take more strain than nature intended. Poor posture can lead to chronic back pain and injuries, joint problems, and even can affect the position and functions of your vital organs.

When you slouch over, lean to one side, or lock your joints, you are placing the burden of your weight on your joints instead of your muscles. When you stand up straight and unlock your joints, your muscles assume your weight in a safe manner.

How does this relate to working out? Always try to keep your back tight and upright when lifting weights, or picking things up. When you round your back, your spine assumes the burden of the weight that you are lifting. When you hold your back straight and tight, the muscles around the spine will take the weight. This will allow you to lift more weights, which should provide for better results in the weight room. This will also reduce the risk of injury while lifting weights.

There are several keys to practicing good posture. Start by making a conscience effort to stand up straight most or all of the time. Try to sit up straight when at work, church, or other times that you sit for an extended period of time. Stretching, yoga, and pilates can help posture. Also, try to strengthen your core muscles through abdominal and lower back exercises. A strong core will go a long way in posture improvement. Improving your posture is a good way to improve your quality of life. You will look better, feel better, and your self-confidence will improve. Good posture even burns more calories than slouching. When we get tired, we slouch and lock our joints, but when we stand up straight, we have to use our muscles, which will help us get stronger *and* burn more calories. Poor posture often results from a lifetime of bad posture habits, but it is never too late to try to improve it. It may take a while to develop posture "habits," but you can make good posture a habit. The earlier you start, the better off you will be.

CHAPTER EIGHT

Are Your Kids Fit? The Importance of Youth Exercise

Statistics show that there are more unfit, overweight, and obese children today than there have ever been. One in five children in the U.S. is overweight and one in six is considered seriously overweight. Obese children are reported to have a 70 percent likelihood of obesity continuing into adult years.

How can you combat this problem? Start by teaching your kids to be active. Daily activity, such as sports and play-time, along with exercise, will help create an active lifestyle for your children. Help your children develop healthy fitness and nutritional habits. Physically active children have fewer chronic health problems and are at less risk of develop-ing cancer, diabetes, heart disease, and high blood pressure. Staying fit will also help children develop high self-esteem and improve social interaction.

What are some good exercises for children? Sports and games are always good activities. Strength training is also very important for children. Many people keep their chil-dren away from strength training because of fear that it will stunt growth or alter muscle and bone development. The claims of strength training stunting growth and develop-ment are false. Countless studies have shown that strength training, when done properly, has no adverse effects on the growth and development of young bodies. Many studies have actually shown that strength training in youth is not only very good for them, but in many instances is safer than sports play. Improved muscle strength in children has many benefits, including, less joint pain and injury, stronger bones, improved athletic performance, higher metabolism, and im-provements in the way they look and feel.

Children of all ages should be active in some form. Children can strength train as long as they are supervised and do it correctly. Children can do bodyweight resistance exercises like push ups, pull ups, and sit ups, or they can use resistance bands to create light resistance. They can also use free weights and machines with light weights when supervised. Children should do full body workouts that incorporate high reps, light weights, and good, safe form.

If you need help with supervising your children's exercise or help with appropriate routines for them, then seek the help of a personal trainer or physical education teacher. Your children are building the foundation for the rest of their lives. Help them build a good healthy foundation that will lead to a lifetime of health and fitness. Remember, *you* are your children's best role model, so lead by example, get out there and start exercising with your kids today!

CHAPTER NINE

Make an Investment in Your Health

People spend time and money on things that are important to them. Isn't your health important? If you have to invest a little time and money for your health, it will pay off. Take a look at the big picture. Take a look at the long-term benefits. Hire a personal trainer. I have provided some workouts in this book, but it is always good to spend some time with a trainer to learn form and intensity. Having a personal trainer is also very good for accountability and discipline. If time restraints are a problem, then take a look at your overall daily activities, cut something else out of your daily routine, and replace it with exercise. Remember, *nothing* is more important than your health! Make a commitment to yourself and to your loved ones to prevent health problems by taking better care of yourself.

CHAPTER TEN

Workout Plans

The workout plans in this section are all effective and when done correctly and consistently, can be very effective. That being said, these are only a few of many, many, different workouts. If you have another workout that you follow, chances are that it may work also. If you are not sure, then seek the advice of a trainer to see if you are doing the right workout for you. While there are many good workouts out there, there also are a lot of bad ones too, so double check to make sure that yours is right for you. Most of the workouts listed in this book need to take place in a gym because of the variety of equipment, but there will be an in-home option to follow for those of you who need it. All of the workouts are complete and include every muscle group.

TO BE SAFE, ALWAYS CONSULT YOUR DOCTOR BEFORE BEGINNING A NEW PROGRAM. FOLLOW THESE WORKOUTS AT YOUR OWN RISK.

General Workout Plan (two-day plan)

This workout can be used by just about anyone regardless of size, age, gender, goals, or any other characteristic. You can do this plan as many times per week as you want; alternate days every time you workout. You will never do the same body part on consecutive days, so there is room for rest on this plan. Do three or four sets of ten to fifteen reps on each exercise. Start with a medium weight and do fifteen reps on the first set. Try to increase the weight on each set and aim for ten to fifteen reps each set. Some of the exercises have more than one choice. The choices are for variety. Pick one exercise on the ones that have multiple options.

Day 1
1. Abs – Knee Raise
2. Abs – Incline Sit Ups
3. Chest – Chest Press Machine or Dumbbell Chest Press
4. Chest – Chest Fly Machine or Dumbbell Chest Fly
5. Back – Lat Pull Downs or Pull Down Machine
6. Back – Seated Row or Row Machine
7. Legs – Dumbbell Squats or Smith Machine Squats
8. Legs – Leg Extensions
9. Legs – Walking Lunges or Step-Back Lunges

Day 2
1. Abs – Leg Raises (on a bench)
2. Abs – Crunch Machine
3. Shoulders – Shoulder Press Machine or Dumbbell Shoulder Press
4. Shoulders – Dumbbell Front Raise
5. Shoulders – Dumbbell Side Raise
6. Triceps – Cable Pushdowns or Bench Dips

7. Biceps – Dumbbell Curls or Curl Machine
8. Legs – Leg Press (plate-loaded) or Leg Press (pin-select machine)
9. Legs – Seated Calf Raise or Calf Raise on the Leg Press
10. Legs – Inner Thigh Machine
11. Legs – Outer Thigh Machine

General Workout (three-day plan)

This plan is good for males or females and can be used as many days per week as needed. Do three to four sets of each exercise and eight to fifteen reps. Increase the weight each set and decrease reps.

Day 1
1. Abs – Knee Raise
2. Abs – Incline Sit Ups
3. Shoulders – Dumbbell Shoulder Press or Machine Shoulder Press
4. Shoulders – Dumbbell Front Raise
5. Shoulders – Dumbbell Side Raise
6. Shoulders – Dumbbell Rear Raise or Rear Delt Machine
7. Legs – Leg Extensions
8. Legs – Seated Leg Curls or Laying-Down Leg Curls
9. Legs – Inner Thigh Machine
10. Legs – Outer Thigh Machine

Day 2
1. Chest – Chest Press Machine or Dumbbell Chest Press
2. Chest – Chest Fly Machine or Dumbbell Chest Fly
3. Back – Lat Pull Downs or Pull Down Machine
4. Back – Seated Row or Row Machine
5. Biceps – Dumbbell Curls or Curl Machine
6. Lower Back – Low Back Extensions or Low Back Machine

Day 3
1. Abs – Leg Raises
2. Abs – Ab Crunch Machine
3. Triceps – Bench Dips or Dumbbell Overhead Triceps Press
4. Triceps – Cable Pushdowns (metal bar or rope)
5. Legs – Dumbbell Squats or Smith Machine Squats
6. Legs – Leg Press (plate-loaded or pin-select)
7. Legs – Seated Calf Raises or Calf Raise on the Leg Press
8. Legs – Lunges (any type)

General Workout (four-day plan)

This workout can be done by anyone, regardless of goals. Weight and reps can be altered depending on your goals. This workout covers the major body parts two times per week.

Monday: Chest, Back, Shoulders, Abs
1. Chest – Bench Press or Dumbbell Press
2. Chest – Incline Bench Press or Dumbbell Incline Press
3. Back – Any Pull Down or Pull Ups
4. Back – Any Back Row
5. Shoulders – Military Press or Dumbbell Shoulder Press
6. Shoulders – Shoulder Press Machine
7. Abs – four sets of any ab exercises

Tuesday: Legs and Arms
1. Legs – Regular Squats or Smith Machine Squats
2. Legs – Leg Extensions
3. Legs – Calf Raises
4. Biceps – Standing Straight Bar Curls
5. Triceps – Nose-breakers
6. Biceps – Preacher Curls
7. Triceps – Cable Pushdowns (with metal bar)

Wednesday: Rest

Thursday: Chest, Back, Shoulders
1. Chest – Chest Press Machine
2. Chest – Chest Fly Machine or Dumbbell Fly

3. Back – Chin Ups or Close-Grip Pull Downs or One-Arm Dumbbell Row
4. Traps – Dumbbell Shrugs or Straight-Bar Shrugs
5. Lower Back – Extensions or Machine
6. Shoulders – Standing Dumbbell Shoulder Press
7. Shoulders – Dumbbell Front Raise
8. Shoulders – Dumbbell Side Raise

Friday: Legs, Arms, Abs
1. Legs – Leg Press
2. Legs – Seated Leg Curls or Laying-Down Leg Curls
3. Legs – Inner and Outer Thigh Machines
4. Biceps – Cable Curls
5. Triceps – Bench Dips
6. Biceps – One-Arm Concentration Curls
7. Triceps – Cable Pushdowns (with the rope)
8. Abs – four sets of any ab exercises

Express Workout Plan

This workout is for individuals who have limited time. Don't let "not enough time" be an excuse anymore! These workouts can be completed in thirty minutes or less. This workout puts the most emphasis on important, effective, exercises, and covers every muscle group through two different workouts. This workout also includes some super-set exercises. It is fast-paced and will build muscle and burn calories. Use this one as many times per week as you can, alternating each workout each day. Do three sets of eight to twelve reps on everything.

Day 1
1. Incline Sit Ups Superset with Knee Raises
2. Chest Press Superset with Lat Pull Downs
3. Chest Fly Superset with Seated Row
4. Standing Dumbbell Shoulder Press
5. Shoulder Front Raise Superset with Side Raise
6. Lower Back Extensions Superset with Crunches

Day 2
1. Ab Crunch Machine Superset with Leg Raises
2. Leg Press or Squats Superset with Calf Raises
3. Leg Extensions Superset with Leg Curls
4. Standing Straight Bar Arm Curls
5. Dumbbell Overhead Triceps Press
6. Bicep Curl Machine Superset with Cable Triceps Pushdowns

Mass Building Workout

This workout is for people who want to lift for growth. As far as lifting goes, you can gain muscle mass from this workout, but remember, to grow more, you have to eat more. You have to eat for growth. This workout is a five-day split and works each muscle group once per week. The goal is to work the muscles very hard and let them recover until the next week. The sets and reps vary on per exercise. On each exercise, increase weights each set and decrease reps.

Day 1: Chest and Abs
1. Bench Press: five sets of four to ten reps
2. Dumbbell Chest Press: four sets of four to ten reps
3. Incline Chest Press: four sets of four to ten reps
4. Chest Fly: three sets of ten to twelve reps
5. Knee Raises: two sets of fifteen to twenty reps
6. Incline Sit-ups: two sets of fifteen to twenty reps
7. Crunch Machine: two sets of fifteen to twenty reps

Day 2: Back
1. Lat Pull Downs or Pull Ups: four sets of six to ten reps
2. Seated Row: four sets six to ten reps
3. Close-Grip Pull Downs or Pull Down Machine: four sets six to ten reps
4. Row Machine or One-Arm Dumbbell Row: four sets of six to ten reps
5. Lower Back Extensions: three sets of ten to fifteen reps

Day 3: Legs
1. Squats: four sets of six to ten reps
2. Leg Press: four sets of six to ten reps

3. Leg Extensions: four sets of eight to twelve reps
4. Leg Curls: four sets of eight to twelve reps
5. Calf Raises: four sets of ten to fifteen reps

Day 4: Shoulders
1. Military Press: four sets of six to ten reps
2. Dumbbell Shoulder Press: four sets of six to ten reps
3. Front Raises: three sets of eight to twelve reps
4. Side Raises: three sets of eight to twelve reps
5. Rear Delts: three sets of eight to twelve reps
6. Shrugs: four sets of eight to fifteen reps

Day 5: Arms
1. Standing Straight Bar Curls: four sets of eight to twelve reps
2. Nose-breakers: four sets of eight to twelve reps
3. Preacher Curls: four sets of eight to twelve reps
4. Cable Triceps Pushdowns w/ Metal Bar: four sets of eight to twelve reps
5. One Arm Concentration Curls: three sets of eight to twelve reps
6. Cable Triceps Pushdowns w/ Rope: three sets of ten to fifteen reps

Functional Workout

This workout can be done every day, every few days, or every now and then to break up the regular routine and shock your body. Try to go back-to-back on everything and not rest too much.

1. Thirty Jumping Jacks
2. Body Weight Squats (Do ten reps then hold at the bottom for ten seconds, then do ten more reps and a ten-second count, then, ten more reps and a ten-second count, all without resting)
3. Push Ups: as many as you can
4. Pull Ups: as many as you can
5. Medicine Ball Lunges: fifteen each leg (use dumbbells if you don't have a medicine ball)
6. Exercise Ball Shoulder Press: thirty reps (sit on an exercise ball and do dumbbell shoulder press)
7. Squat-Curl-Press-Press: fifteen reps (use a kettle bell or medicine ball for this. Start by holding the weight in front of you and squat down and up, then do an arm curl with the kettle bell, then shoulder press it and hold it in the pressed position, then tricep press it behind your head. That is one rep)
8. Sit Ups: thirty to fifty reps
9. Plank: thirty seconds

Repeat everything above two more times

Youth Workout

There are many ways for kids to exercise. The following workout could help kids, ages ten to thirteen get in better shape. As always, consult your doctor and make sure the child does not have any health problems or reasons that they shouldn't start exercising. For kids thirteen or older, or who are more physically mature, they can try the regular workouts listed in this book. This workout can be done two to four times per week. Each exercise should be done for three sets of ten reps, using light to medium weight.

1. Chest Press Machine or Push Ups
2. Lat Pull Downs or Pull Down Machine
3. Seated Row or One-Arm Dumbbell Row
4. Standing Dumbbell Shoulder Press
5. Body Weight Squats
6. Box Jumps
7. Dumbbell Arm Curls
8. Cable Triceps Push Downs
9. Incline Sit Ups
10. Crunches
11. Standing Calf Raises
12. Side Twists (with a medicine ball or broom handle)

Golf Workout

There are many different ways for golfers to workout. The problem that I see with many "golf" workouts is that they focus too much on the golf-specific exercises. The golfer never really develops appropriate strength through traditional regular exercises. Sometimes golfers are scared to do traditional exercises because they fear that they will get too big or lose their flexibility. That is not the case. If you never get stronger, the specific golf exercises will not help. My golf workouts include regular traditional exercises and golf-specific movements. I use the traditional exercise for the golfer to get in better shape and gain strength, and I use the golf-specific exercises to help specifically with golf movements. Take a look at the most in-shape golfers on tour today. These golfers workout a lot harder than you would think, and do a lot more traditional exercise than you would think. Don't limit yourself to one training style. Be open minded and train completely.

Do three sets of ten to fifteen reps on each exercise and alternate days as many times per week as you can.

Day 1
1. Bench Press or Exercise Ball Press
2. One-Arm Cable Chest Fly or Dumbbell Fly
3. Lat Pull Down or One-Arm Cable Row from the Top
4. One-Arm Dumbbell Row or One-Arm Cable Row from the Middle or Bottom
5. Standing Dumbbell Shoulder Press or Shoulder Press Sitting on an Exercise Ball
6. Dumbbell Front and Side Raises (superset)

7. Incline Sit Ups
8. Lower Back Extensions
9. Side Twists with a Broom Handle (standing or sitting)
10. Good Mornings with a Broom Handle (hold the handle behind your head at the top of your back and while looking forward, bend over forward to almost a ninety-degree angle and then straighten back up)
11. Upper Body Stretching
12. Assisted Hamstring Stretching (let someone stretch you a little further than you can on your own)

Day 2

1. Leg Press or Squat Machine
2. Leg Extensions
3. Seated Leg Curls
4. Standing Dumbbell Biceps Curls
5. Cable Triceps Pushdowns
6. Overhead Cable Triceps Press
7. Standing Calf Raises
8. Kettle Bell Squats
9. Kettle Bell Arm Curls
10. Medicine Ball Lunges with a Twist at the Bottom
11. Side Throws with a Medicine Ball
12. Kettle Bell Straight-Leg Deadlift (hold the kettle bell in front of you and lower to your toes and back while stretching your hamstrings)
13. Incline Sit Ups or Ab Crunch Machine
14. Medicine Ball Take Aways (mimic a golf backswing to both sides)
15. Assisted Hamstring and Leg Stretching

Sports-Specific Workouts

These sports-specific workouts are a combination of traditional exercises and functional exercises. *Remember, if you don't get stronger through regular exercises, the sports training will not be as effective.* Do Both!

Football

This workout is a three-day split and can be done two times per week with a rest day in the middle. The reps vary on each exercise. Try to go as heavy as you can within the rep range, safely, and without sacrificing form. (Note: learn, as early as possible, the proper squat form. It will save you from injury and make you stronger in the long run.)

Day 1
1. Bench Press: four sets of eight to twelve reps
2. Pull Ups (pull downs if you cannot pull up): three sets of eight to twelve reps
3. Standing One-Arm Dumbbell Row (athletic position): three sets of eight to twelve reps
4. Incline Dumbbell Chest Press: three sets of eight to twelve reps
5. Push Ups: two sets of twenty to thirty reps
6. Lower Back Extensions: two sets of ten to twenty reps
7. Standing Straight-Bar Arm Curls: four sets of eight to twelve reps
8. Cable Triceps Pushdowns: four sets of eight to twelve reps
9. Upper Body Stretching

Day 2

1. Squats: four sets of eight to twelve reps
2. Dead Lifts: three sets of eight to ten reps
3. Standing Military Press: four sets of eight to twelve reps
4. Dumbbell Shrugs: three sets of ten to fifteen reps
5. Leg Extensions: three sets of ten to fifteen reps
6. Seated Leg Curls: three sets of ten to fifteen reps
7. Seated Calf Raise: three sets of ten to fifteen reps
8. Dumbbell Front Shoulder Raise: two sets of fifteen reps
9. Dumbbell Side Shoulder Raise: two sets of fifteen reps
10. Leg and Shoulder Stretching

Day 3

1. Dips: three sets of ten to fifteen reps
2. Clean and Press: three sets of five to ten reps
3. Incline Sit Ups (with a partner throwing medicine ball): three sets fifteen
4. Knee and Leg Raises (back laying on bench): two sets of thirty reps
5. Side Twists with a Medicine Ball: two sets of thirty reps
6. Box Jumps: three sets of fifteen reps
7. Parking Lot Sprints: sprint twenty-five yards and walk back; repeat ten times
8. Partner Squat Throws (Stand six to eight feet from your partner, in a parallel-level squat position. Throw a medicine ball back and forth ten times without moving your lower body): three sets

Day 4
Rest
Baseball

Do this workout four to six times per week alternating each day

Day 1

1. Bench Press: three sets of ten to twelve reps
2. Chest Fly: three sets of ten to twelve reps
3. Lat Pull Downs or Pull Ups: three sets of ten to twelve reps
4. Seated Row or Standing One-Arm Dumbbell Row: three sets of ten to twelve reps
5. Bicep Curls (any type): three sets of ten to twelve reps
6. Cable Triceps Pushdowns: three sets of ten to twelve reps
7. Incline Sit Ups with a Medicine Ball: two sets of fifteen to twenty reps
8. Lower Back Extensions: two sets ten to fifteen reps
9. Medicine Ball Twists: two sets of thirty reps
10. Crunches (on the floor): two sets of twenty-five to thirty reps
11. Side Bends (holding a dumbbell): two sets of twenty reps
12. Cable Twists (from middle setting with a straight bar, hold the bar in front of your abdomen and twist your torso from front to one side without moving your legs): three sets of ten reps to each side

Day 2

1. Dumbbell Squats: three sets of twelve reps
2. Leg Press and Calf Raises: three sets of ten to twelve reps each
3. Leg Extensions: three sets of ten to twelve reps
4. Laying-Down Leg Curls: three sets of ten to twelve reps
5. Standing Dumbbell Shoulder Press: four sets eight to twelve reps
6. Dumbbell Side Raise: two sets of fifteen reps
7. Dumbbell Front Raise: two sets of fifteen reps
8. Squat Throws (Grab a weighted ball or tennis ball, get in a parallel squat position, and stay down; have someone stand in front of you about five to eight feet away and have them throw you the ball ten times to each hand): three sets each hand
9. Walking Lunges with Twist: three sets of ten lunges each leg
10. Medicine Ball Slams (Stand up straight with the medicine ball and slam it to the ground on each side of your body ten times): two sets of ten on each side
11. Medicine Ball Side Throws (Have a partner stand ten feet away, face them at your side, throw the ball across your mid-section to your partner ten times from each side to generate power from your core): two sets of ten reps on each side

Basketball

Alternate each workout each day and rest one day after completing both workouts.

Day 1

1. Bench Press or Dumbbell Chest Press: four sets of ten to twelve reps
2. Incline Chest Press or Chest Fly: four sets of ten to twelve reps
3. Pull Ups or Lat Pull Downs: four sets of ten to twelve reps
4. Seated Row or Row Machine: four sets of ten to twelve reps
5. Arm Curls (any type): four sets of ten to twelve reps
6. Cable Triceps Push Downs: three sets of ten to twelve reps
7. Dips: three sets of ten to fifteen reps
8. Incline Sit Ups: three sets of fifteen to twenty reps
9. Lower Back Extensions: three sets of ten to fifteen reps

Day 2

1. Squats: three sets of ten to fifteen reps
2. Box Jumps: three sets of ten to fifteen reps (as high as you can safely jump)
3. Standing Military Press: three sets of ten to fifteen reps
4. Seated Dumbbell Shoulder Press: three sets of ten to fifteen reps
5. Leg Extensions: three sets of ten to twelve reps
6. Leg Curls: three sets of ten to twelve reps
7. Jump Squats (Load a squat bar with a lighter weight than you would normally do regular squats with; squat down, explode on the way up, and jump at the top as high as you can safely jump while holding the bar tight to your back): two sets of ten reps

8. Standing Calf Raises with Squat Bar: two sets of twenty reps
9. Dumbbell Front Shoulder Raise: three sets of fifteen reps
10. Dumbbell Side Raise: three sets of fifteen reps
11. Crunches: two sets fifty reps
12. Knee and Leg Raises: two sets each of twelve to fifteen reps

At-Home Workout

This workout is designed to do with as little equipment as possible. Invest in a 25 to 50 lb dumbbell set and an exercise ball. Alternate each workout each day.

Day 1
1. Push Ups or Dumbbell Chest Press on the Ball: three sets of ten to fifteen reps
2. Dumbbell Chest Fly on the Ball: three sets of ten to fifteen reps
3. Standing One Arm-Dumbbell Row: four sets of ten to fifteen Reps
4. Dumbbell Shoulder Press (standing or seated on the ball): three sets of ten to fifteen reps
5. Dumbbell Front Shoulder Raise: three sets of ten to fifteen reps
6. Dumbbell Side Shoulder Raise: three sets of ten to fifteen reps
7. Dumbbell Rear Delt Raise: three sets of ten to fifteen reps
8. Lower Back Extensions on the ball (Lay face down, rounding over the ball with your mid-section, put your hands behind your neck with your elbows out or just cross your chest, raise your chest and shoulder up from the ball until your lower back tightens): three sets of ten to twelve reps
9. Exercise Ball Crunches: three sets of twenty to thirty reps

Day 2
1. Dumbbell Squats: four sets of ten to fifteen reps
2. Dumbbell Lunges: three sets of ten each leg

3. Dumbbell Straight-Leg Dead-Lift: three sets of ten to fifteen reps
4. Standing Calf Raises with Dumbbell (Stand on the edge of a step.): four sets of ten to fifteen reps
5. Standing Dumbbell Arm Curls: four sets of ten to fifteen reps
6. Triceps Dips (Use a chair or a bench.): four sets of ten to fifteen reps
7. Floor Crunches or Sit Ups: three sets of ten to twenty reps
8. Exercise Ball Leg Lifts (Laying on the floor on your back, grip the ball with your feet and raise the ball off of the ground as far as you can go.): three sets of ten to twenty reps

Traveling? – On the Road Workout

If you are traveling and don't have access to any dumb-bells or a ball, then you can purchase workout bands that are very compact and have different levels of resistance. You can loop the bands around furniture or your own body to create resistance variations. You can follow a similar plan as the "At-Home Workout" above, just replace the dumbbells with the bands. The bands will usually come with illustrations on how to do each exercise. If you do not have any bands, you can always do push ups, sit ups, jumping jacks, body-weight squats, and lunges.

CHAPTER ELEVEN

Workout Summary

All of the workouts that I have provided can be very useful and can produce optimum results—if you work hard! These workouts can be used by males *and* females. These workouts are just a few that can be effective; there are many more workouts that are also effective as well. The bottom line is that you need to be doing something and these can help. Although there are many great workouts out there, there are also many bad ones. If you are not sure about your current workout, then consult a trainer and find out if it is helping you or hurting you. It is also good to consult a trainer and make sure that your form is safe and effective. Remember to work hard, but work safe, and always, **perform the workouts at your own risk.**

VI.
SUPPLEMENTS

To Take or Not to Take

Have you ever looked at a fitness or exercise magazine and noticed all of the ads for supplements, and then closed the magazine more confused than ever? If you are like most people, you want results and you want them now! Often times, supplements are seen as a faster way to get these results. People will take supplements along with a sub-par workout regimen and a poor diet and think that they will see results. The first thing that needs to be pointed out is the fact that if you are not exercising and eating well, then supplements will be useless. Your first goal should be to do a correct workout, lift hard, do your cardio at an intense level, and eat to accommodate your exercise. You will see a great amount of results from doing these things. You can actually get years of results from constant improvement of your weight training, cardio, and diet. When your results slow down, then you may want to look into supplements.

With supplements, keep it simple. Try to stick to the basics—protein, caffeine, energy drinks, and possibly creatine.

Protein is what your muscles use to grow. The most popular protein supplements are shakes and bars. You can also increase your protein intake by eating more meat with your meals. If you lift weights, then you probably need to increase your protein intake.

Caffeine and energy drinks can give you energy and increase your metabolism. You will use the extra energy to get better workouts. Caffeine works by increasing your heart rate, so if you have a heart condition or any reason that your heart rate should not be elevated, then you should consult a doctor before having caffeine or energy drinks. Remember to choose the energy drinks that are low carb, which will be low in sugar and calories.

Creatine occurs naturally in the body and supplies energy to muscle and nerve cells. Creatine can increase strength and speed and can help with muscle recovery. Short-term use of creatine in normal doses taken by healthy people is generally considered safe and has not been linked to any adverse side effects. It would be a good idea to drink lots of water while taking creatine to help keep your kidneys flushed and hydration levels high. As always, if you are not sure whether you should take creatine or not, consult a doctor.

Try not to waste your time with NANO-VIPER-CREA-OXIDE-EXPLOSION- type supplements that are found in all the magazines. They are usually nothing more than a waste of money. Try to get your diet and exercise where they need to be and then stick to the basics; your results will fall in place!

VII.
MY DIET AND EXERCISE HISTORY

Practice what you preach.

I did not eat the way that I do today five years ago. I didn't eat the way that I did five years ago ten years ago. And so on, and so on…. My diet has evolved over the years. I feel that I have always eaten fairly well, but I have also always improved my diet. I have walked up the steps that I spoke about earlier in this book for literally the past twenty years.

It had to start somewhere!

My childhood was very active. I would play until dark every day, come in and eat dinner, and sometimes go out again to play. (I believe I may be the last generation that spent literally every afternoon playing outside.) I also have ridden off-road motorcycles since I was five years old. In addition to riding motorcycles, I played basketball, rode and raced BMX bikes, rode road bicycles, and skateboarded regularly. Needless to say, I was an active kid. Like most kids of my generation, childhood obesity was not a possibility because we were so active and because we also ate the majority of our meals at home. I am a part of the last "non-fast-food" generation. Three square meals, a snack here and there, and *lots* of activity kept me in good shape for my childhood years.

In high school, I continued to be very active while I ate a ton of food. I was so active that no matter how much I ate, I never gained weight. I stayed very lean because I worked out and played two to four hours of basketball ever day. I briefly started lifting weights in middle school, but it wasn't until my freshman year of high school, at the age of fourteen, that I started what would become a lifetime of lifting weights and the foundation of a healthy lifestyle. I remember it as if it was yesterday—being in the high school weight room and doing some bench presses. I was able to bench press 135 lbs. For those of you who don't think much of bench presses, 135 lbs is the weight where you have a 45 lb weight on each side. It is the first "landmark" in bench pressing (and I could lift it). That day, I became obsessed with bench presses and remained obsessed for at least the next fifteen years. High school for me was basketball and weight lifting. Over those four years, I really got into working out as a hobby, or even as a sport. I learned everything about lifting weights that I could, usually from magazines or watching other people at the local gym. My "situation" in high school can be listed as weight training via working out, cardio by playing basketball, and no real diet direction at all.

College was the first segment of my life that I started changing things up a little. I started improving my situation. I was able to put on a little weight. That being said, if I wanted that weight to be muscle and not fat, then I had to go about it the correct way. I played basketball basically everyday in college and it covered most of my cardio, but I still tried to run every now and then for some extra cardio. My weight lifting continued to grow. My strength and knowledge grew tremendously during my four years of college. Those four years are where I really started learning and practicing different workout splits and covering the entire body over different days. This also allowed my muscles to "rest" for the first time ever. The rest, along with being over eighteen years old—and finally a little more prone to gain—enabled me to put on a good 5 lbs of muscle each of the four years of college. Those four years are when my diet started to evolve as well. When college began, I had no rules on diet, which meant that I ate whatever I wanted, whenever

I wanted. By the second year of college, I implemented my first rule/step. That rule was that I had to eat one healthy meal per day, and the rest of the time I could eat whatever I wanted. (I had no idea at the time that this was the first step in a lifetime of steps!) By the end of college, I had taken the next step, which was that I could have one cheat meal per day and the rest of the day had to be healthy. Basically, it was a flip-flop of rule number one. I started college at 155 lbs and about 5 or 6 percent body fat. I graduated college four years later at 175 lbs still at about five or six percent body fat—a gradual, progressive improvement!

My early adult life, when I was in my early to mid twenties, was a time of tremendous improvements on my diet and weight training. This was also when I started personal training and really educating myself on diet and exercise. When I was twenty-three, I was working full time and going to the gym for two hours everyday after work. I was practicing the idea of making exercise "part of my day." My diet had evolved into a four- to five-day week of good eating and two to three days of cheating on the weekends. My cardio had not improved much during this time. I played basketball once or twice per week and that was about all. I stayed lean because of my diet improvements and because of how often and how hard I lifted weights. This time period was also when I gained the most muscle mass of my life and I was the strongest I have ever been. My weight increased to about 195 lbs and I could bench press 385 lbs and squat 405 lbs. I never got "huge" or became a "meathead," but I definitely was a workout freak!

During my late twenties to present day (at the time of writing this book, I am thirty-four years old), was when my diet and exercise evolved even more and toward the goal of being as lean as I possibly could while still enjoying life—the foundations and principles that are taught in this book. My workouts have stayed fairly extensive, but have evolved over the years to more efficient and sometimes functional work-outs. I do still lift hard and heavy, but at a faster pace. My diet and cardio have evolved the most during this time. My cardio has grown over the past eight or nine years from once per week to five to six times per week. I very rarely miss cardio. Over those same eight or nine years, I have gradually cut calories out of my diet. What was once a plan of eating good Monday through Thursday, having about 3000 to 4000 thousand calories per day during those days, and cheating three meals per day on the weekends has evolved into twelve to fifteen hundred calories per day Monday through Friday and cheating maybe one time per day on the weekends. I currently have a really good "situation" of cardio, weight training, and diet going, and it is producing consistent results and keeping me happy. My situation can be described like this: Lift to get big, cardio to get lean, and eat for both! As my results slow, I just work harder to produce more results. When I reach a point where I can't work any more or any harder, then I will change up my routine. The steps to success have been a part of my life for over twenty years now. I will keep climbing them forever. It's a progressive, lifetime plan!

Working Out (2008)

"Most Fit" Photo Shoot (2008)

VIII.
Final Thoughts
(For Now at Least!)

This chapter contains my final thoughts on a progressive system of diet and exercise. That being said, with my diet and exercise forever improving in a gradual way, there will probably be future books with even more helpful information. So, these are my final thoughts…for now at least!

There are several key ideas to take from this book. One of them is to keep things simple. Work hard enough to get results, but not so hard that you quit. There are some diet and exercise terms and ideas that you did not see in this book and you might be wondering where they are—Glycemic index, Max VO2, Resting Metabolic Rate, Fast Twitch and Slow Twitch, and probably many more. There are several details to diet and exercise that are good to know, but at many levels it can be unnecessary. Chances are you can get great results without worrying about confusing terms like those listed above. Keep it simple, work hard, and eat better! You don't have to be a fitness freak or a health nut to make improvements. You can do it and still be a normal person.

No results are ever guaranteed, but if you make positive changes, then there is no reason that you shouldn't achieve results. Ultimately, it is up to you! The information in this book can work. I have used it to make over twenty years of gradual improvements on my clients and myself. Have a plan, a good plan, just as you would for life, church, sports, work, or anything else important to you. Your health and wellness needs a plan. Get things organized. ANYTHING is possible if you have a plan.

Your body is a temple. Take care of it. Find a balance in life. Do as much good for yourself as you can while still enjoying life. If you work so hard that you are miserable, then you need to readjust. Is it worth it if you are miserable?

Probably not, so back off a little, look at the big picture, and find a balance of working hard and being happy.

I am a big proponent of reading and educating in all aspects of life. I really enjoy self-help books. Some of the self-help books that I read have no direct help with health, but the principles can be applied to diet and exercise. Start reading and educating yourself in all aspects. Become a better person. Clean up your life. Improve all aspects of your life. Improve your health. Become a better parent, friend, spouse, and so on. Work harder at your job. Get out of debt. Become a better you. All of these things will work together; similar principles can be applied to improve all aspects of your life.

-Don't be a slave to anything. You can beat it. Whatever it is that is holding you back, you can beat it.

-*You* have the ultimate power. Look yourself in the mirror and tell yourself that it is time to change and that you can do it.

-Failure is not an option if your motivation is strong enough.

-Life is more rewarding when you work hard. Work hard; play hard; enjoy life!

-Don't be lazy. Change your mental state. So much of your energy is affected by your mental perception.

These are just a few examples of hundreds of thoughts that are important to live by. They can be applied to any aspect of your life, especially diet and exercise. You take care of the things that you love. Love yourself. Take care of yourself!

ACKNOWLEDGEMENTS

First off, I would like to thank God. Without God, *nothing* is possible. Although it has taken many years of reading, note-taking, and careful planning to gain the material for this book, I could not have done any of it, especially putting the pen to the paper without God. I really want to thank God for my experiences in life that have shaped me—for my drive, for believing failure is not an option, and for my organizational skills (which border OCD!)—all of which made this book go from a dream to a reality. Most importantly, I want to thank God for giving us a manual to live by, the Holy Bible, and for giving us an eternal role model, his son, Jesus Christ.

I would also like to thank my dad, mom, and stepfather for teaching me the right ways of life, for never pushing me in a direction that I didn't want to go, for allowing me to be independent with my learning and decision making, and for always supporting me…no matter what! I would not be where I am today without you.

Thank you to my wife for giving me my two angels, Palmer and Peyton, and for being a fitness role model herself. She is in great shape, has competed in fitness competitions, ran track and cross country in college, and continues to run and workout religiously. I have an amazing family!

Thank you to everyone that has influenced my fitness career. Especially, Russ Yeager, David Ferrell, Buster Prader, Evan Slaughter, and every other workout partner I have ever had. Thank you Buster for showing me how to lift heavy!

Thank you to my brother and to all of my family and friends. I have the best friends in the world and I hope that at some time, I have helped, or will someday help, you improve your health and life.

Thank you to everyone that bought this book. You have made a great step in changing your health and improving your life!

Sources:

Health Problems listed in the "Preventative Health" section: **U.S. Department of Health and Human Sciences**

Osteoporosis statistics and information: **NOE.org** and **About.com**

Posture statistics and information: **American Physical Therapy Association**

Youth Exercise statistics and information: **American Council on Exercise, mayoclinic.com**